THIRD EDITION

Academic Writing Course

STUDY SKILLS IN ENGLISH

Longman

R.R. Jordan

Pearson Education Limited
Edinburgh Gate, Harlow,
Essex CM20 2JE England
and Associated Companies throughout the World

www.longman.com

This edition published by Pearson Education Limited 1999
Sixth impression 2003

ISBN 0582 40019 8

Produced for the publishers by Bluestone Press, Charlbury, Oxfordshire, UK
Design: Gregor Arthur; Keith Rigley at White Horse Graphics (this edition)
Printed in Spain by Graficas Estella

Acknowledgments
For the third edition of this book, I am very grateful to a number of people
for ideas and suggestions. In particular, members of the British Association
of Lecturers in English for Academic Purposes (BALEAP) were most helpful:
June O'Brien, John Morley, Ian Pople, Pauline Robinson, Penny Adams,
Jo McDonough, Lou Lessios, Mark O'Reilly, Alan Barr, Moira Calderwood,
Esther Daborn, Esther J. Dunbar, Tony Dudley-Evans. From Australia:
Mary Cole, Cathy Pegolo, Christine Bundesen. In addition: Chris Keeble,
David Preen, Jane Jordan.

I am grateful to my editors for their advice and co-operation at all stages:
Kate Goldrick at Longman and, especially, Andy Hopkins and Joc Potter of
Bluestone Press for their detailed editing.

By the same author:
English for Academic Purposes: A guide and resource book for teachers-
Cambridge: Cambridge University Press, 1997

For BALEAP members

Contents

Guide to Using the Book

The Aim of the Course

1 To enable non-native speakers of English who wish to follow a course in the medium of English at tertiary level to express themselves coherently in writing.

2 To provide samples of academic writing and appropriate practice material for such students and also for those students who need to write essays or reports in English at an intermediate to advanced level.

3 To act as a revision course for students who have previously learned English as a foreign language at school and who probably learned English with the sentence as the grammatical unit. These students may now need to write in English for academic purposes.

4 To provide some practice in answering examination-type questions for public or internal exams.

The Organisation of the Course

Units

The book is divided into units that are self-contained but are linked in their progression through the overall needs of students who have to write in English for an academic purpose.

Many of the units focus on language functions that are used to express a particular notion or idea, e.g. description and definitions. The procedures of academic writing are also practised, e.g. paraphrasing and summarising. The most common genre (type of writing) that is practised is the essay. However, some practice is also provided in writing for exams, and information is given about writing research reports.

Written practice is given at different levels within each unit, mostly in three stages. All the units except the first conclude with a Structure and Vocabulary Aid to provide assistance with the words and grammatical constructions needed in that unit.

Key

The Key at the end of the book provides additional comments on some of the exercises and gives answers to many of the exercises.

Appendices

The Appendices act as a bank of reference material for both the student and the teacher. Appendix 1 provides an overview of some of the common types of language error and their causes. It also lists some useful books that give further practice in these areas.

Product and Process

Overall, the course provides practice in writing for a particular purpose: often models or examples are given from academic writing. In addition, the process of achieving the final product is considered. Students are encouraged to discuss and compare some of their writing, and to draft and check their writing carefully through proofreading. The teacher's use of a correcting code (Appendix 4) will help in this respect.

Using the Book

It is best if the units are worked through in order. However, this depends on the requirements of the students, who may need to practise the content of certain units before others (for example, Unit 14: Academic Style). The Structure and Vocabulary Aids should be referred to when necessary. Normally, the answers to each exercise should be checked in the Key before proceeding to the next exercise.

Suggestions for the Teacher

General

1 In a number of units there are blank-filling exercises to be done after reading a text. These can be used with some flexibility: students who have difficulty can look at the text again or at the same time as they are writing. Other students can do the exercises without referring back to the text. Advanced students can try to do the exercises before looking at the text. In other words, they will be trying to anticipate or predict the language needed from the context of the sentence.

2 Students may need to practise different kinds of academic writing (genres) in preparation for their studies of a particular subject. Units 14 and 16 will be particularly useful for this. In addition, it would be helpful if they could see examples of essays, reports, etc. of the type they will need to write in the future. Information about the requirements and expectations of subject departments would be particularly useful.

3 Some groups of students may be studying the same academic subject, e.g. one of the sciences or social sciences. If this is the case, then it would be helpful if you could devise some questions related to their specific subject at the end of Stage 3 for each unit. Similarly, some students may be at undergraduate level while others may be postgraduates. Consequently, practice at the appropriate level would be beneficial.

4 The questionnaires in Unit 17 and Appendix 5 may be photocopied for students to complete.

5 As a learning resource for students, any word processing package can help them to edit their own texts. There are also a range of websites which give access to learning and practice material (guidance, models, examples).

Examination Practice

Some students may need to practise writing answers for examination questions, either for internal or public exams. For such practice they need to be able to analyse the questions and decide what is needed. In addition, they need to write concisely, fluently and accurately. Unit 19 will be especially useful for this: its Glossary of Examination and Essay Questions will be generally useful for writing essays. Other units that are useful for exam practice are numbers 11–15.

One feature of writing for exams is the need to be able to write quickly – 'against the clock': for example, one essay-type question in one hour. Practice for this can be devised by giving a certain time limit in which to write some of the Stage 3 exercises, particularly those that apply to the students' own subject.

If a class is formed of students from the same subject area, it would be useful to obtain copies of past exam papers in their subject. The questions can be analysed with the students, noting the question-types that appear frequently. A question can be selected, discussed, the structure agreed upon and notes put on the board to help the students. They could then be given a time limit to write the answer. Later in the course, the notes on the board can be removed after discussion so that gradually help is reduced.

If the students are of mixed disciplines, they can be asked to provide questions about their own subjects. After suitable preparatory work they can attempt to write the answers under simulated exam conditions.

It is also possible to obtain information about public exams with examples of question papers. For example, *The IELTS handbook* is available from UCLES, Cambridge. Information about these exams, as well as other aspects of academic writing, is given in *English for Academic Purposes* (A guide and resource book for teachers) by R. R. Jordan, Cambridge University Press, 1997.

Correcting Code

Sometimes when checking students' writing, it is necessary to write in the correct answers. However, some research has shown that if students are actively involved in trying to correct their own mistakes, with guidance, they are more likely to learn from them and not repeat them. One way to help in this respect is to use a code for correcting (see Appendix 4). With this approach, mistakes are not corrected but are indicated – both the type of mistake and its location.

Where a student's writing is 'good' or 'very good', it is very helpful to the student if you can indicate which parts are good and briefly explain why they are. Without such comments, students may not repeat the good features in their next writing.

In addition to the Correcting Code, an appropriate Checklist for the type of writing (e.g. essay) can be constructed. If this is also circulated to students it will raise their awareness of what is needed and also remind them of what to check for. It can be used in conjunction with Unit 18. Examples of its content might be:

– Relevance of the answer to the question or topic
– Structure and organisation of the essay, and completeness of the writing

- Clear expression
- Coherence of argument
- Critical evaluation of points of view
- References to literature/research and use of quotations and bibliography
- Other details: grammar, spelling, punctuation

Discussion and Writing

Several discussion activities have been included, and students are encouraged to compare and discuss their answers with other students. The purpose is to raise the level of awareness of students of certain aspects of written English. In addition, the discussion is a useful prelude to writing discussion-type essays in which points of view need to be argued. It helps in the evaluation of differences between arguments. Such discussion also helps to develop critical thinking and self-confidence in expressing one's own views.

Pyramid Discussions

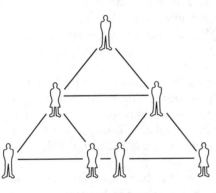

A Pyramid Discussion is an activity in which students are encouraged to take part in discussion by gradually increasing the size of the discussion group, starting with the individual, then building up to two students, then four, and then the whole group. The procedure is as follows:

1 First, students should individually select three items, as instructed, from the list given in the activity. The order of their choices is not important.

2 Then each student, in turn, should call out the numbers of his/her choices. Write these on the board for all to see.

e.g. student:	A	B	C	D etc.
choices:	12	3	4	1
	14	7	7	7
	15	10	12	10

3 After this, put the students in pairs so that they have, as far as possible, at least one choice in common (e.g. A and C, B and D above).

4 In pairs the students should then try to persuade each other to make changes in their choices so that at the end of a certain time limit (perhaps five minutes) they both agree on three choices. If necessary, they can compromise on new choices or 'trade-off' choices. The pairs' three choices are then noted on the board again.

5 Pairs should then be placed together who have at least one choice the same . . . and so the procedure continues until all of the class are involved.

6 If a pair or group finish their discussion before other groups, they can prepare arguments to defend their choices so that they are ready to meet another group.

7 While they are discussing, students will be practising the language of persuasion: agreement, disagreement, suggestion, qualification and compromise.

8 At the end of the activity is a suggestion that students can add some items of their own to the list. This may be done in pairs instead of, or in addition to, individually.

Pyramid Discussions are included in the following units: 2, 6, 7, 8, 11, 12, 15, 17 and 19. In addition, you could compose your own lists for extra topics, perhaps with the students suggesting items for the list (consisting of about 10–15 items). If more information is needed about Pyramid Discussions, see *ELT Journal*, Vol. 44 No. 1, January 1990, Oxford University Press ('Pyramid Discussions' – R. R. Jordan, pages 46–54).

Advice for the Student

With academic writing it is particularly important that you should check to ensure that it has the appropriate formal style. Help is given with this in Unit 14. General difficulties are covered in Unit 18 and Appendix 1. Appendix 1 also refers to some books that can help you with further practice in areas of general difficulty.

The Pyramid Discussion in Unit 2 Stage 3 contains a list of advice that should help to improve your academic writing. To that list could be added the need to write at least two drafts before you write the final version. Each draft should be revised after leaving it for a day or more so that you can think about and check any difficulties that you have.

If it is possible, you will find it very helpful to see examples of the type of writing that you are aiming to prepare for, for example, essays and reports. If the examples are good ones, they will show you the structure of the writing, the formal style, and the referencing system.

Unit 1   Structure and Cohesion

This unit is concerned with the general organisation of a piece of academic writing (e.g. a report, an essay, an assignment, a project), its structure and particularly the way in which the different parts are linked together. The plan below of a piece of writing, in this case an essay, will help to explain the overall structure.

Stage 1
Structure

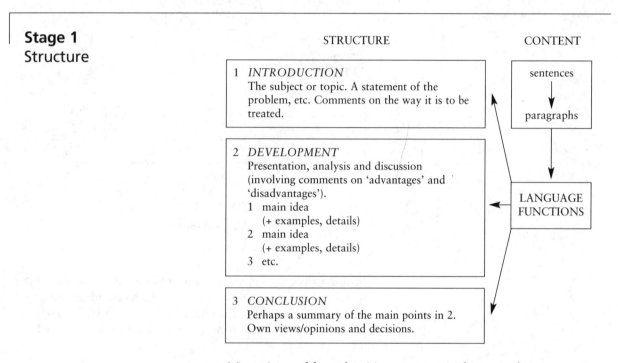

STRUCTURE

1 *INTRODUCTION*
The subject or topic. A statement of the problem, etc. Comments on the way it is to be treated.

2 *DEVELOPMENT*
Presentation, analysis and discussion (involving comments on 'advantages' and 'disadvantages').
1 main idea
    (+ examples, details)
2 main idea
    (+ examples, details)
3 etc.

3 *CONCLUSION*
Perhaps a summary of the main points in 2. Own views/opinions and decisions.

CONTENT

sentences

↓

paragraphs

LANGUAGE FUNCTIONS

Most pieces of formal writing are organised in a similar way – introduction; development of main ideas or arguments; conclusions. Each part of the writing will consist of language functions: particular uses and structures of the language organised according to the specific purpose that the writer has in mind in wishing to communicate ideas etc. to other people – describing, defining, exemplifying, classifying etc.

Each language function consists of sentences and/or paragraphs that are joined together or linked by connectives (words or phrases that indicate a logical relationship). These language functions will be examined in detail in the following units. In the rest of this unit we shall look at the linking of sentences by means of connectives.

Stage 2
Connectives

A piece of writing or text will often have the following structure:

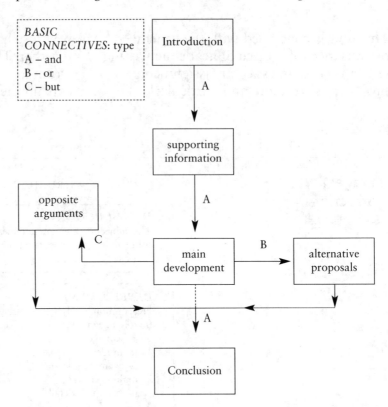

BASIC CONNECTIVES: type
A – and
B – or
C – but

A The discussion, argument, or comment in the development of the topic may be very straightforward, in which case ideas will be added together one after the other. The basic connective *and* is used here. (A number of connectives have a similar or related meaning to *and*.)

B Sometimes the comments may be expressed in another way, or an alternative proposal may be made. This is represented by the basic connective *or*. (A number of other connectives have a similar meaning.) After the alternative has been considered, the main argument will continue.

C There are also occasions in arguments etc. when the opposite is considered or referred to. This is represented by the basic connective *but*. (There are also a number of other connectives with a similar meaning.) After the opposite or opposing view has been considered, the main argument is continued.

A list of the connectives divided into the main groups of *and, or, but* is contained in Appendix 2: Connectives.

1 'And' type: Connectives of Result (Type A)

Look at the following example:

He passed his examinations;	*so,* *therefore,* *as a result,* *accordingly,* *consequently,* *thus,* *hence,*	he had some good news to tell his parents.
Because he passed his examinations,		

> **Note:** The connectives (in *italics*) join a cause ('he passed his examinations') with a result, effect or consequence ('he had some good news to tell his parents').

Add a second sentence. Use a suitable connective from the list above, and a result, effect or consequence from the list below.

a   Many students find it difficult to read newspapers in English . . . _____

_____

b   Most students living abroad are interested in news of their own country . . . _____

_____

c   When a student goes abroad to study he/she may have to complete about twelve different forms . . . _____

_____

Result, Effect or Consequence:

. . . British news is found to be of most interest.
. . . they usually read the international news first in the newspapers.
. . . an average of five books per month are read.
. . . not many read one regularly.
. . . it is useful to be able to answer questions briefly.

Complete the following by adding a suitable ending of your own.

d   The lecture was very difficult to understand. Consequently,

_____

e   Carlos was only able to read very slowly in English. Therefore,

_____

2 'Or' type: Connectives of Reformulation (Type B)

Look at the following example:

He said that he had kept the library book for several years.	*In other words* *To put it more simply,* *It would be better to say*	he had stolen it.

> **Note:** The connectives (in *italics*) introduce a reformulation of what has come before. The reformulation appears in different words and is used to make the idea clearer or to explain or modify it.

Add a second sentence. Use a suitable connective from the list above, and an appropriate reformulation from the list below.

a   Maria is rather slow at learning . . . _____

_____

b   Helen finds languages quite easy . . . _____

_____

c   Anna speaks English like a native-speaker . . . _____

_____

Reformulation:

. . . she speaks it excellently.
. . . she speaks slowly.
. . . she is taking a long time to improve her English.
. . . she has little difficulty in learning English.
. . . she speaks it with great difficulty.

Complete the following by adding a suitable ending of your own.

d   Margaret is bilingual. In other words, _____

_____

e   Some people say that if you are good at music you will also be good at learning languages. In other words, _____

_____

3   'But' type: Connectives of Concession (Type C)

Look at the following example:

The time available for discussion was very limited.	*However,* *Nevertheless,* *Nonetheless,* *Yet,* *In spite of that,* *All the same,*	it was still possible to produce some interesting arguments.

> **Note:**   The connectives (in *italics*) indicate the surprising nature of what follows in view of what was said before; a kind of contrast is indicated.

Add a second sentence. Use a suitable connective from the list above, and a concession (or contrast) from the list below.

a   Some of the examination questions were very difficult . . .

_____

_____

b   There was only limited money available for research . . .

_____

_____

c   The project was very complicated . . . _____

_____

Concession:

... Dimitrios was not able to do it.

... Juan succeeded in completing it in time.

... Abdul was able to obtain a grant.

... Oscar did not manage to complete them.

... Ali managed to answer them satisfactorily.

Complete the following by adding a suitable ending of your own.

d It seemed likely that he would fail the test. However,

_____

e There were a number of good reasons why he should not finish the experiment. Nevertheless, _____

_____

Stage 3
Paragraphs

It is essential to divide your writing into paragraphs. A paragraph normally contains several sentences but they are all concerned with the theme contained in the topic or key sentence (i.e. the main sentence). The key sentence is usually the first one, which contains the main idea or topic. The other sentences support it by adding further information or examples. A paragraph is self-contained but should link logically with the previous and following paragraphs so that the flow and cohesion of the writing is maintained.

1 Look at the paragraph at the end of Stage 1. Which is the key sentence?

2 The following sentences are in mixed order. To form a paragraph they need to be reorganised. Underline the key sentence and put the sentences in the correct order by numbering them 1–5.

a It is mainly formal, impersonal and objective.

b In most of these the writer is expected to include references to other writing or research.

c Academic writing is a particular kind of writing that can be recognised by its style.

d These include essays, research reports and articles, case studies, surveys, dissertations, theses, and examination papers.

e Other distinctive features will depend upon the specific types of academic writing.

Note: Paragraphs are either indented from the left margin (i.e. they start further in from the left) or a line of space is left at the end of a paragraph and the next paragraph is started on the left margin. This makes it easier for the reader to read a text.

Unit 2   Description: Process and Procedure

When we describe a process or procedure, we often use present passive verb forms (*is/are* + verb stem + *ed* e.g. *it is manufactured*) to give a general description.

When we report a particular procedure, we are concerned with only one particular occasion in the past; then we often use the past passive tense (*was/were* + verb stem + *ed* e.g. *it was heated*).

A description that does not involve a process or procedure is often written in the present simple active tense (verb stem + *s* e.g. *it comprises*).

Sequence, or order, is important in both describing a process or reporting a procedure.

Stage 1
General Description

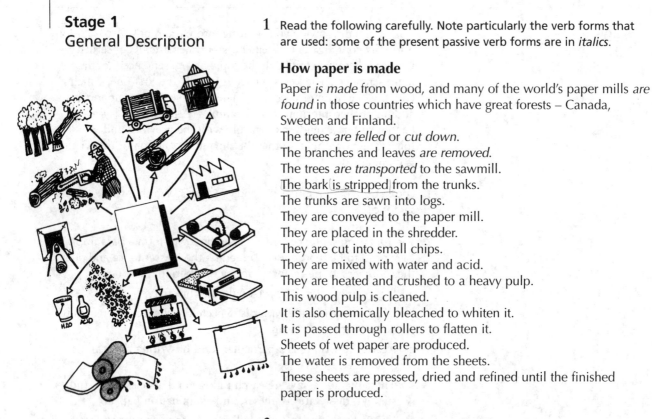

1 Read the following carefully. Note particularly the verb forms that are used: some of the present passive verb forms are in *italics*.

How paper is made

Paper *is made* from wood, and many of the world's paper mills *are found* in those countries which have great forests – Canada, Sweden and Finland.
The trees *are felled* or *cut down*.
The branches and leaves *are removed*.
The trees *are transported* to the sawmill.
The bark is stripped from the trunks.
The trunks are sawn into logs.
They are conveyed to the paper mill.
They are placed in the shredder.
They are cut into small chips.
They are mixed with water and acid.
They are heated and crushed to a heavy pulp.
This wood pulp is cleaned.
It is also chemically bleached to whiten it.
It is passed through rollers to flatten it.
Sheets of wet paper are produced.
The water is removed from the sheets.
These sheets are pressed, dried and refined until the finished paper is produced.

2 Read carefully through the text again and <u>underline</u> other present passive verb forms.

Note:	1 When describing a process, sequence markers, e.g. *first, then, next, finally* . . . are often used (see Appendix 2: Connectives, Section 1). They help to link the sentences.
	2 Sometimes, in order to avoid repeating a subject, a relative pronoun and relative clause are used, e.g. *The bark is stripped from the trunks. The trunks are sawn into logs* becomes *The bark is stripped from the trunks, which are sawn into logs.*

3 Some of the sentences from the text have been joined together below to form a paragraph. Spaces have been left in the sentences. In the spaces write an appropriate verb (and sometimes preposition), and, if suitable, a relative pronoun.

First, the logs _____ in the shredder. Then they
_____ into small chips _____ water and acid.
Next they _____ to a heavy pulp _____.
It _____ also chemically _____ to whiten it.
After this, it _____ through rollers to flatten it. Then,
sheets of wet paper _____. Finally, the water
_____ from the sheets _____ until the
finished paper _____.

4 Look at the sequence of pictures below. Underneath there are a number of sentences describing how a breakfast cereal is made. The sentences are in the wrong order. Write them out in the correct order using the sequence of pictures to help you.

How a breakfast cereal is made

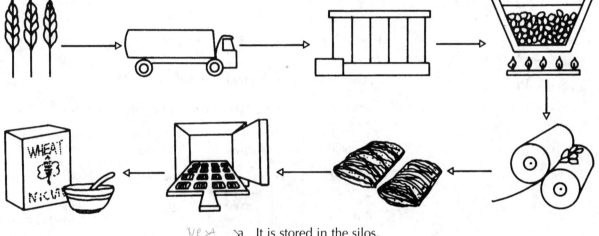

Next   a It is stored in the silos.
            b These are woven into biscuits.
First   c The wheat is harvested from the field.
            d Each biscuit is baked until brown.
then   e It is cut and formed into thin strips.
Afterthis   f The grain is cooked to soften it.
            g It is packed ready to be eaten.
then   h The wheat grain is transported to the silos.

5 Look carefully at the diagram on page 16 of the stages of manufacture of glass bottles. Six boxes have been numbered and left empty. Now read carefully the sentences next to the diagram. They are in the wrong order and are not complete.
– Complete the sentences by putting the verb (given at the end of each sentence) in the appropriate passive form.
– Write the sentences in the correct order.
– Join them together by means of sequence markers (e.g. *then, next*).
– Finally, from the information in the sentences, write the correct names in the six boxes in the diagram.

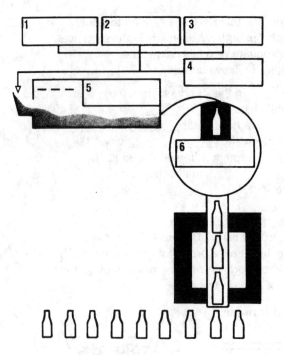

How glass bottles are made

a It _____ into bottles in the mould. (shape)

b Sometimes broken glass _____. (add)

c The bottles _____ to strengthen the glass. (reheat and cool)

d Glass _____ from sand, limestone, and soda ash. (make)

e They are ready _____. (use)

f Glass _____. (produce)

g This mixture _____ strongly in a furnace. (heat)

h These three materials _____ together in the right proportions. (mix)

Stage 2
Specific Procedure

1 Look at the following table carefully.

Writing in English: Manchester University (50 students)

% students	type of writing	(average) frequency	(average) length
52	essay	5 per term	2000 words
34	report	2 per term	4000 words
14	dissertation	1 per year	8000 words
12	thesis	1 after 2–3 years	300–1000 pages

The information in the table can be described (as an alternative to using the table). Notice the construction of the following sentence:

52% of the students wrote essays, *of an* average frequency *of 5* per term, *of an* average length of 2000 words.

Now read the following paragraph, which describes some of the information contained in the table. Complete the spaces with information from the table.

A survey was conducted among _____ overseas postgraduate students at _____. The purpose of the survey was to discover the type, _____ and _____ of academic writing that was expected of the students by their supervisors or tutors. _____ of the students _____ reports, of an _____ 2 per term, _____ average length _____.

2 Below the steps or stages in conducting a survey are given. In the spaces in each sentence write an appropriate verb from the following list. Use past passive forms of the verbs, e.g. *was/were asked*.

Verbs: request, collect, carry out, publish, analyse, distribute

a A survey _____ among 50 students.
b First, questionnaires _____ to the students.
c Then the students _____ to write answers to the questions.
d After this, the completed questionnaires _____.
e Next, the answers _____.
f Finally, the results _____.

> **Note:** See Unit 17 for conducting an actual survey.

Stage 3
Advice

1 Read carefully the following description of the procedure for writing an essay. It gives advice in the form of what you *should* do. (Most of the verbs are modal passive forms, e.g. *should* + passive infinitive.) When you have finished reading do the exercise in 2.

The Stages of Writing an Essay

First, the topic, subject or question should be thought about carefully: what is required in the essay should be understood. Then a note should be made of ideas, perhaps from knowledge or experience. After this, any books, journals, etc.
5 should be noted that have been recommended, perhaps from a reading list or a bibliography. Then to the list should be added any other books, articles, etc. that are discovered while the recommended books are being found.

Now is the time for the books, chapters, articles, etc. to be
10 read, with a purpose, by appropriate questions being asked that are related to the essay topic or title. Clear notes should be written from the reading. In addition, a record of the sources should be kept so that a bibliography or list of references can be compiled at the end of the essay. Any
15 quotations should be accurately acknowledged: author's surname and initials, year of publication, edition, publisher, place of publication, and page numbers of quotations.

When the notes have been finished they should be looked through in order for an overview of the subject to be obtained.
20 Then the content of the essay should be decided on and how it is to be organised or planned. The material should be carefully selected: there may be too much and some may not be very relevant to the question. The material, or ideas, should be divided into three main sections for the essay: the introduction,
25 the main body, and the conclusion. An outline of the essay should be written, with use being made of headings or sub-headings, if they are appropriate.

The first draft should be written in a suitably formal or academic style. While doing this, the use of colloquial

30 expressions and personal references should be avoided. When it has been completed, the draft should be read critically, and in particular, the organisation, cohesion, and language should be checked. Several questions should be asked about it, for example: Is it clear? Is it concise? Is it comprehensive? Then

35 the draft should be revised and the final draft written – legibly! It should be remembered that first impressions are important.

Finally, the bibliography should be compiled, using the conventional format: the references should be in strict alphabetical order. Then the bibliography should be added to the end of the essay.

2 All the sentences containing advice (*should*) are listed below. Spaces have been left for the verbs. In each space write the appropriate verb, but write it as a direct instruction (putting the verb in its imperative form) e.g. *should be finished* → *finish*.

The Stages of Writing an Essay

a _Think_ carefully about the topic, subject or question.

b _Understand_ what is required in the essay.

c _Make_ a note of your ideas, perhaps from your knowledge or experience.

d _Note_ any books, journals, etc. that have been recommended, perhaps from a reading list or a bibliography.

e _Add_ to your list any other books, articles, etc. that you discover while finding the recommended books.

f _Read_ the books, chapters, articles, etc. with a purpose, by asking yourself appropriate questions that are related to the essay topic or title.

g _Make_ clear notes from your reading.

h _Keep_ a record of your sources so that you can compile your own bibliography or list of references at the end of your essay.

i _Acknowledge_ accurately any quotations: author's surname and initials, year of publication, edition, publisher, place of publication, and page numbers of quotations.

j _Look_ through your notes when you have finished in order to obtain an overview of the subject.

k _Decide_ on the content of your essay and how you want to organise it, in other words, plan it.

l _Select_ your material carefully: you may have too much and some may not be very relevant to the question.

m _Divide_ your material, or ideas, into three main sections for the essay: the introduction, the main body, and the conclusion.

Summary of the Stages of Writing an Essay

1. Topic — think
   Reading list

2. *Ideas - of ideas*

3. *Make a list of notes, books journals*

4. *Read chapter journals, books with purpose Ask question*

5. *Make notes on keep reference, question*

6. *Extract from the notes and decide the*

7. *outline.*

n   *Write*   an outline of the essay, making use of headings or sub-headings, if they are appropriate.

o   *Write*   the first draft, in a suitably formal or academic style.

p   *Avoid*   the use of colloquial expressions or personal references.

q   *Read*   the draft critically, in particular checking the organisation, cohesion and language.

r   *Ask*   yourself several questions about it, for example: Is it clear? Is it concise? Is it comprehensive?

s   *Revise*   the draft.

t   *Write*   the final draft.

u   *Make*   sure it is legible!

v   *Remember*   first impressions are important.

w   *Complete*   your bibliography, using the conventional format.

x   *Make sure*   that your references are in strict alphabetical order.

y   *Add*   the bibliography to the end of your essay.

3 Read through 'The Stages of Writing an Essay' again. Decide what you consider to be the most important stages or advice. In very brief note form summarise the stages by filling in the boxes in the diagram. The first one has been done for you (you may change it if you do not agree with it).

Either: Before beginning, discuss with the student next to you what you both consider to be the most important stages. Do you agree with each other?

Or: After you have finished, compare your summary diagram with the student next to you and discuss any differences.

Pyramid Discussion
Writing an Essay or Report

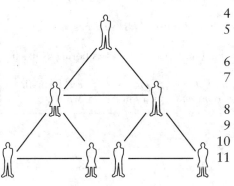

Individually select the three most important pieces of advice, from the list below, that you think will help to improve a student's academic writing. The order of the three choices is not important.

1 Write precisely: clearly, accurately and explicitly.
2 Use correct language: grammar, vocabulary, spelling etc.
3 Organise the writing carefully: introduction, main body, and conclusion.
4 Write legibly: handwriting should be easy to read.
5 Write in an academic style: impersonally, without using colloquial language.
6 Write concisely, and avoid very long sentences.
7 Adopt appropriate attitudes: be rational, critical, honest and objective.
8 Carefully paragraph the writing.
9 Include variety in the writing: avoid too much repetition.
10 Check details carefully, both of content and of language.
11 Ensure that the opening paragraph is not too long and that it creates a good impression.

12 Pay as much attention to the conclusion as to the introduction.
13 Avoid the use of clichés, jargon, propaganda, exaggeration, and emotive language.
14 Ensure that ideas and items are arranged in a logical sequence and are logically connected.
15 Always acknowledge the source of quotations and paraphrases.

Finally add some advice of your own that is not covered in the list above.

> **Note:** Information about organising a Pyramid Discussion in the classroom is given in the Guide to Using the Book.

Structure and Vocabulary Aid

A Commonly used verb tenses, with examples

Present Simple (Active)	Present Simple (Passive)
it carries/they carry	*it is carried/they are carried*

Past Simple (Active)	Past Simple (Passive)
it carried/they carried	*it was carried/they were carried*

Modal Passive	Imperative/instruction
it should be given/they should be given	*give*

B Relative pronouns and relative clauses

1 *Who/that* refers to persons.
2 *Which/that* refer to things.
3 *Whose* refers to the possessive of persons.
4 *Whom* refers to persons and is often used with a preposition.

Examples:
1 My supervisor, *who seems very young*, has just been promoted to head of department.
2 The article *which* (or *that*) *I have just finished reading* is very clearly written.
3 The research *that* (or *which*) *I finished last year* has just been published.
4 The lecturer *whose name I always forget* was as boring as usual this morning.
5 The student *with whom I share a room* is very noisy [formal].
The student *I share a room with* is very noisy [informal].

Unit 3   Description: Physical

In academic writing, physical description may occur in a number of disciplines or subjects. A description of people, family relationships, occupations and institutions might occur in social or physical anthropology or sociology. A description of apparatus and equipment might occur in the various sciences. For nearly all these descriptions present simple active verb forms (e.g. *she wears/they wear*) and present simple passive verb forms (e.g. *it is described/ they are described*) are commonly used. The following stages concentrate on describing countries.

Stage 1
The United Kingdom

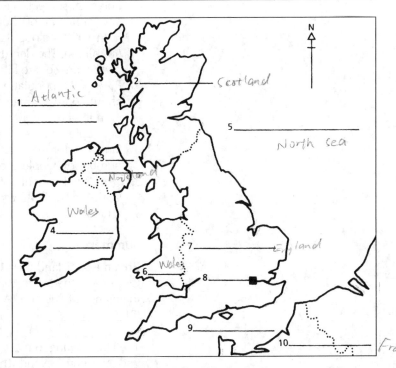

1 Read the following paragraph carefully. Write the names of the places next to the numbers in the map.

The United Kingdom

Britain (or Great Britain) is an island that lies off the north-west coast of Europe. The nearest country is France, which is 20 miles away and from which Britain is separated by the English Channel. The island is surrounded by the Atlantic
5 Ocean to the west, and the North Sea to the east. It comprises the mainlands of England, Wales and Scotland, that is, three countries. Scotland is in the north, while Wales is in the west. Ireland, which is also an island, lies off the west coast of Britain. It consists of Northern Ireland and the Irish
10 Republic. Britain together with Northern Ireland constitute the United Kingdom (UK). Thus, the United Kingdom is

composed of four countries, the largest of which is England. The capital city is London, which is situated in south-east England.

2 Now read the second part of the text. When you have finished, complete the summary below of the whole text by using appropriate verb forms. Sometimes a preposition is needed as well.

15 The UK has a total area of about 244,100 square kilometres (94,248 square miles). About 70% of the land area is devoted to agriculture, about 7% is wasteland, moorland and mountains, about 13% is devoted to urban development, and 10% is forest and woodland. The northern and western
20 regions of Britain, that is Scotland and Wales, are mainly mountainous and hilly. Parts of the north-west and centre of England also consist of mountains and hills.

Britain has a generally mild and temperate climate. It is, however, subject to frequent changes. It has an average
25 annual rainfall of about 120 centimetres (47 inches).

In 1998 the population of the United Kingdom was nearly 59 million. The density of population was approximately 240 people per square kilometre. However, in England, where 83% of the population live, the density was much higher,
30 about 363 per square kilometre.

In the UK, English is the first language of the vast majority of people. However, in western Wales, Welsh is the first language for many of the people. In Scotland only a small number of people speak Gaelic.
35 In Britain about 66% of the population say that they are Christian, while fewer than 5% say that they belong to other religions.

Summary

Britain is an island that (1) _____ the Atlantic Ocean and the North Sea. It (2) _____ the mainlands of England, Wales and Scotland. Ireland (3) _____ the west coast of Britain. It (4) _____ Northern Ireland and the Irish Republic. The United Kingdom (5) _____ Britain together with Northern Ireland. The capital city is London which (6) _____ south-east England.

In 1998 the population of the UK (7) _____ nearly 59 million. The density of population (8) _____ 240 people per square kilometre. In the UK English (9) _____ the first language of most people. In western Wales, Welsh (10) _____ many of the people, but few people in Scotland (11) _____ Gaelic.

Stage 2
Other Countries

1 Look carefully at the map of Australia and at the table of information. Then write a description of Australia organised in a similar way to the description of the UK. Check the Structure and Vocabulary Aid if necessary. Write four short paragraphs on:
>   location
>   size and physical background
>   climate
>   population, language, and religion

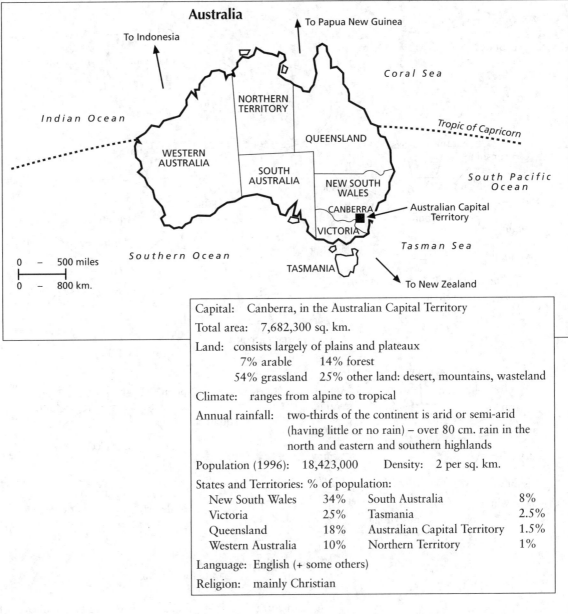

Australia

To Indonesia

To Papua New Guinea

Coral Sea

Indian Ocean

Tropic of Capricorn

NORTHERN TERRITORY

QUEENSLAND

WESTERN AUSTRALIA

SOUTH AUSTRALIA

NEW SOUTH WALES

South Pacific Ocean

CANBERRA

Australian Capital Territory

VICTORIA

Tasman Sea

Southern Ocean

0 – 500 miles

0 – 800 km.

TASMANIA

To New Zealand

Capital:	Canberra, in the Australian Capital Territory

Total area: 7,682,300 sq. km.

Land: consists largely of plains and plateaux
      7% arable   14% forest
      54% grassland   25% other land: desert, mountains, wasteland

Climate: ranges from alpine to tropical

Annual rainfall: two-thirds of the continent is arid or semi-arid (having little or no rain) – over 80 cm. rain in the north and eastern and southern highlands

Population (1996):   18,423,000   Density: 2 per sq. km.

States and Territories: % of population:

New South Wales	34%	South Australia	8%
Victoria	25%	Tasmania	2.5%
Queensland	18%	Australian Capital Territory	1.5%
Western Australia	10%	Northern Territory	1%

Language: English (+ some others)

Religion: mainly Christian

2 Now write a brief account of your country, divided into four paragraphs as above. If you do not know the exact figures, guess or write in general terms.

3 Describe your home town so that the reader, who does not know it, can get a clear picture of it.

Structure and Vocabulary Aid

A Vocabulary: Countries

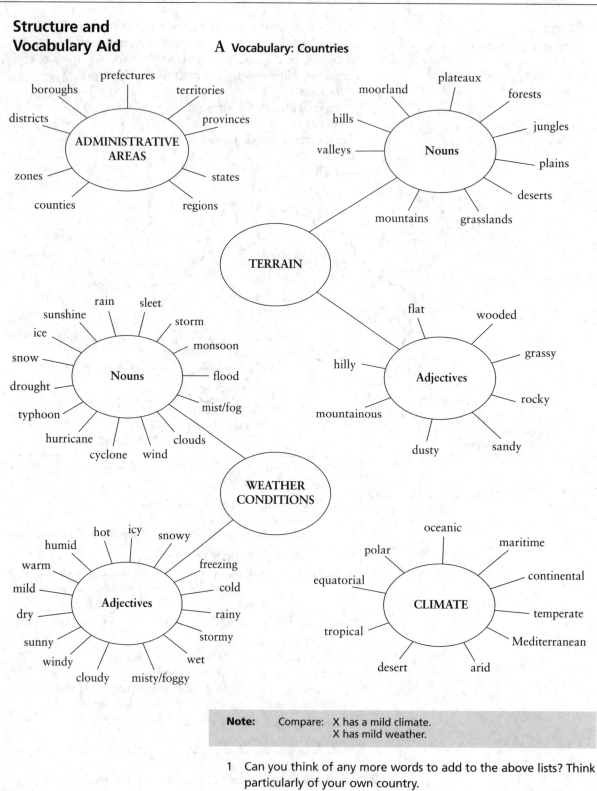

Note: Compare: X has a mild climate.
X has mild weather.

1 Can you think of any more words to add to the above lists? Think particularly of your own country.
2 Are there any more categories or groups of words that you would find useful? If so, try to make lists similar to the above.

B Compass points (and adjectives)

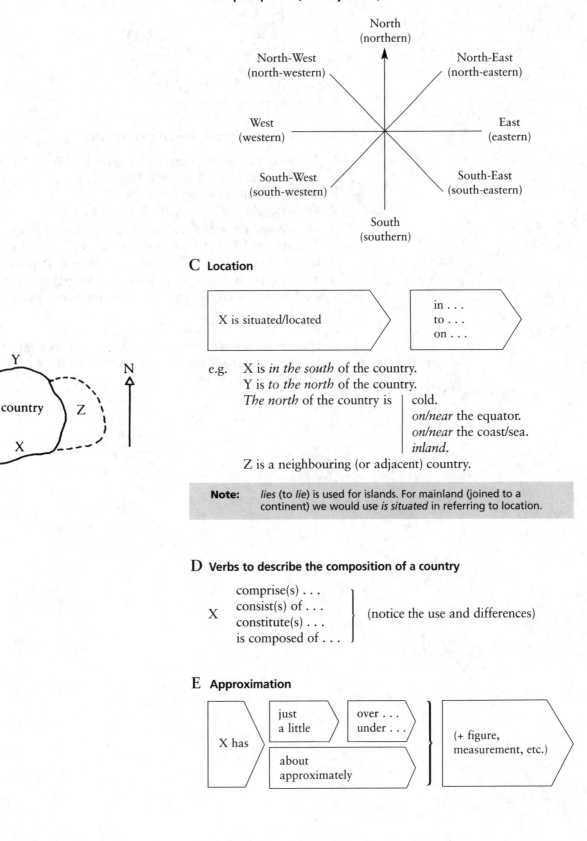

North
(northern)

North-West
(north-western)

North-East
(north-eastern)

West
(western)

East
(eastern)

South-West
(south-western)

South-East
(south-eastern)

South
(southern)

C Location

> X is situated/located

> in . . .
> to . . .
> on . . .

e.g.   X is *in the south* of the country.
Y is *to the north* of the country.
The north of the country is │ cold.
│ *on/near* the equator.
│ *on/near* the coast/sea.
│ *inland.*
Z is a neighbouring (or adjacent) country.

Note: *lies* (to *lie*) is used for islands. For mainland (joined to a continent) we would use *is situated* in referring to location.

D Verbs to describe the composition of a country

X
comprise(s) . . .
consist(s) of . . .
constitute(s) . . .
is composed of . . .
} (notice the use and differences)

E Approximation

X has

just
a little

over . . .
under . . .

about
approximately

} (+ figure, measurement, etc.)

F Qualification

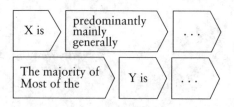

G *The* with names of countries, rivers and seas

1 *The* is **not** used with names of continents (e.g. Europe, not *the* Europe), though it is used with some other geographical areas (e.g. *the* Middle East, *the* Far East).

2 *The* + Republic of . . . (e.g. *the* Republic of France).

3 *The* + country names in the plural (e.g. *the* United States of America, *the* UK, *the* West Indies, *the* United Nations).

4 Other country names are **not** used with *the* (e.g. Denmark).

5 *The* + names of oceans, seas, rivers (e.g. *the* Atlantic Ocean, *the* Mediterranean, *the* Tigris) but **not** with names of lakes (e.g. Lake Baikal).

6 *The* + names of mountain ranges (e.g. *the* Alps, *the* Himalayas). Some individual mountains are named with *the* e.g. *the* Eiger, *the* Matterhorn. In other cases, *the* is **not** used e.g. Mont Blanc, Everest.

Unit 4   Narrative

The introduction to many pieces of academic writing contains some kind of historical background or development. This is usually in the form of narrative: an account or description of events in the past which entails following a time sequence or chronological order (i.e. earliest first). Verb forms commonly used are the simple past active (e.g. *it organised*), simple past passive (e.g. *it was created*), and past perfect active (e.g. *it had developed*).

Stage 1
Dictionaries

1   Read the following carefully. Notice the structure, time sequence, dates, verb forms and prepositions used.

A History of English Dictionaries

The beginnings of English dictionaries date from 1604 when the first 'hard-word dictionary' was published. It contained fewer than 3000 difficult words, which were explained by easier ones. An important principle was introduced: that of
5   listing words in alphabetical order (A–Z).

The first major dictionary was the *Universal Etymological English Dictionary* by Nathaniel Bailey, which was published in 1721. (Etymology is the study of the origin and history of words and their meanings.) This one volume contained about
10   40,000 words.

One of the great landmarks in the history of dictionaries was the publication in 1755 of *A Dictionary of the English Language* by Samuel Johnson. He built on the work of Bailey and illustrated the use of words by including about 100,000
15   quotations from well-known authors from the 16th century onwards. Perhaps his most famous definition is that of 'oats': 'A grain, which in England is generally given to horses, but in Scotland supports the people.'

In America, in 1828, Noah Webster published *An*
20   *American Dictionary of the English Language*. Its two volumes consisted of about 70,000 words and included scientific terms. Webster included American pronunciation and spelling, for example 'color' for 'colour' and 'center' for 'centre'.

25   Probably the most important development in the history of dictionaries was the production of *The Oxford English Dictionary*. Dr James Murray started to edit the enormous work in 1879, and the first part was published in 1884: A – ANT, in 352 pages! It took another 44 years to complete
30   the dictionary, in 125 parts. The final work was published in 1928 in 12 volumes covering 15,487 pages which included nearly 500,000 words.

Samuel Johnson

2   Now make very brief notes of the most important items of information in the passage.

Stage 2
The United Nations

1 Read through the passage below, then write an appropriate word in each of the spaces.

The United Nations (UN)

The _____ of the UN can _____
traced back _____ the League of Nations. This
_____ an international _____ which
_____ created _____ the Treaty of
Versailles _____ 1920 with the purpose
_____ achieving world peace. Before 1930, the
League, from its Geneva headquarters, _____
international conferences and did useful humanitarian work.
_____, it failed _____ deal effectively
_____ international aggression _____
the 1930s. The League _____ formally closed
_____ 1946 and _____ superseded
_____ the United Nations.

    The UN was _____ on 24th October 1945, when
the UN Charter _____ ratified _____
the 51 founder member countries. Almost _____
the countries of the _____ are now members: 185
in all.

    The UN was _____ to maintain international
peace, and to encourage international co-operation to overcome
economic, social, cultural and humanitarian problems. Apart
_____ the _____ organs of the UN
(The General Assembly, The Security Council etc.),
_____ of the UN's work is done _____
its specialised bodies _____ agencies.
_____ of the best _____ are, perhaps,
the FAO, ILO, IMF, WHO, UNESCO and UNICEF.

Discuss possible alternative answers. When the text is complete,
continue with the following exercise.

2 Now make very brief notes of the most important items of
information in the passage.

Stage 3
Universities

1 Below is a passage tracing the development of universities. Read it
through. When you have finished reading it do exercise 2 which
follows the passage.

The Development of Universities

The word 'university' comes from the Latin word 'universitas'
meaning 'the whole'. Later, in Latin legal language 'universitas'
meant 'a society, guild or corporation'. Thus, in mediaeval
academic use the word meant an association of teachers and
5 scholars. The modern definition of a university is 'an institution
that teaches and examines students in many branches of
advanced learning, awarding degrees and providing facilities
for academic research'.

Top: Bologna University
Centre: Vienna University
Bottom: Christ Church College, Oxford

The origins of universities can be traced back to the Middle
10 Ages, especially the twelfth to fourteenth centuries. In the
early twelfth century, long before universities were organised
in the modern sense, students gathered together for higher
studies at certain centres of learning. The earliest centres in
Europe were at Bologna in Italy, for law, founded in 1088;
15 Salerno in Italy, for medicine; and Paris, France, for
philosophy and theology, founded in 1150. Other early ones
in Europe were at Prague, Czechoslovakia, founded in 1348;
Vienna, Austria, founded in 1365; and Heidelberg, Germany,
founded in 1386.
20 The first universities in England were established at Oxford in
1185 and at Cambridge in 1209. The first Scottish university
was founded at St Andrews in 1412. By comparison, the
oldest universities in the USA are at Harvard, founded in
1636, and Yale, established in 1701.
25 In the fifteenth and sixteenth centuries, three more
universities were founded in Scotland: at Glasgow in 1415,
Aberdeen in 1494, and Edinburgh in 1582. The next English
university to be founded was not until the nineteenth century
– London, in 1836. This was followed, later in the nineteenth
30 and early twentieth centuries, by the foundation of several
civic universities. These had developed from provincial
colleges which were mainly situated in industrial areas.
Manchester, for example, received its charter in 1880, and
Birmingham in 1900. In addition, the federal University of
35 Wales was established in 1893 comprising three colleges.
Several other civic universities were founded in the 1940s
and 1950s, such as Nottingham in 1948, Southampton in
1954 and Exeter in 1957. However, it was in the 1960s that
the largest single expansion of higher education took place in
40 Britain. This expansion took three basic forms: existing
universities were enlarged; new universities were developed
from existing colleges; and seven completely new universities
were founded, mostly away from town centres and in the
countryside, e.g. Warwick, 1965. The Open University was
45 founded in 1969: it is non-residential and uses
correspondence courses combined with TV and radio
broadcasts.
A big development in recent years was an Education Act in
1992 that allowed former polytechnics to become universities.
50 Before the Act there were 47 universities in the UK; after the
Act there were 86 universities.
All British universities receive some government funding,
except Buckingham, which is Britain's only independent
university, founded in 1983. This runs two-year courses
55 instead of the usual three years.

2 Below is a summary of the passage in sentences which are given in the wrong order. Put the sentences in the correct order.

a The quarter of a century from 1940 to 1965 was the period when there was a big increase in the number of universities in Britain.

b The Open University was founded in 1969.

c The oldest American university was founded in the seventeenth century.

d One of the original meanings of 'university' was an association of teachers and students.

e There is one private university in Britain: it was established in 1983.

f After three more Scottish universities were established in the fifteenth and sixteenth centuries, the next major developments were not until the foundation of a number of civic universities in the nineteenth and early twentieth centuries.

g Oxford and Cambridge are the oldest English universities.

h Former polytechnics became universities in and after 1992.

i The first Scottish university was established in the early fifteenth century.

j There were gatherings of students at centres of learning in Europe between the twelfth and fourteenth centuries.

3 Now make brief notes of the information relating to the development of English universities only. Put the heading 'Universities in England' above your notes.

4 Write a brief description in narrative form of the development of universities in your country. It does not matter if you do not know precise dates or details: a rough idea or an approximation will be sufficient. Refer to the Structure and Vocabulary Aid.

5 If you apply for a job or to study at a university etc., you normally fill in an application form or send a curriculum vitae (CV). This is a brief account of your background and career. Normally it includes your full name, date of birth, and then, under the heading of 'education', a summary of the secondary schools, colleges or universities that you have attended, together with details of examinations passed and certificates and/or degrees awarded. It is usually followed by an account of your employment or career. The information is normally given in chronological order.

Write part of your own CV. Only include information under the heading of 'education' (places of study and awards).

6 Write a letter to a university or a college applying to study there in the next academic year.

Structure and Vocabulary Aid

A Commonly used verb tenses, with examples

Present Simple (Active)
it created

Past Simple (Passive)
it was established

Past Perfect (Active)
it had developed

B Useful verbs/nouns

verbs
to establish
to create
to found

nouns
establishment
creation
foundation

C Useful vocabulary for describing post-school education

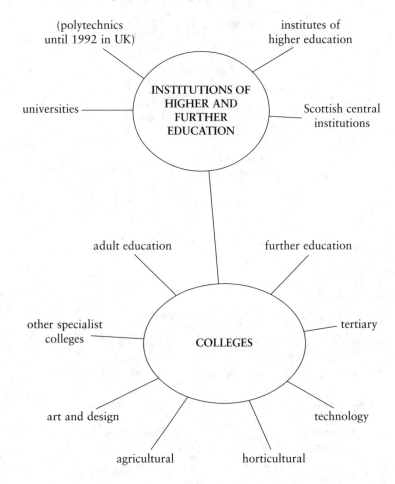

D Useful vocabulary for describing universities

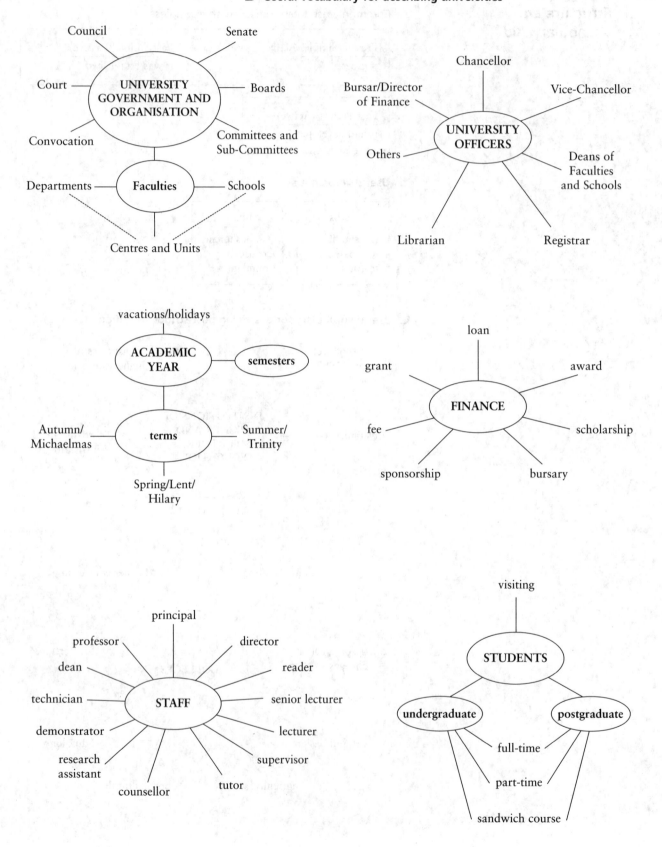

Council

Senate

Court — **UNIVERSITY GOVERNMENT AND ORGANISATION** — Boards

Convocation

Committees and Sub-Committees

Departments — **Faculties** — Schools

Centres and Units

Chancellor

Bursar/Director of Finance

Vice-Chancellor

UNIVERSITY OFFICERS

Others

Deans of Faculties and Schools

Librarian

Registrar

vacations/holidays

ACADEMIC YEAR — **semesters**

Autumn/ Michaelmas — **terms** — Summer/ Trinity

Spring/Lent/ Hilary

loan

grant

award

FINANCE

fee

scholarship

sponsorship

bursary

principal

professor

director

dean

reader

technician — **STAFF** — senior lecturer

demonstrator

lecturer

research assistant

supervisor

counsellor

tutor

visiting

STUDENTS

undergraduate

postgraduate

full-time

part-time

sandwich course

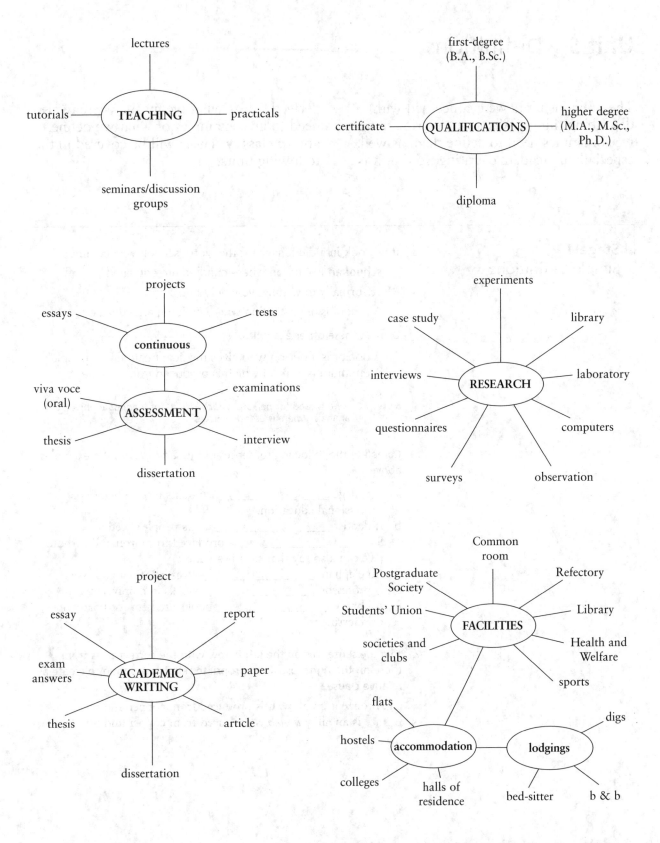

1 Can you think of any more words to add to the above lists?

2 Look at the Academic Writing diagram. Make a list of words for Academic Reading in the same way.

Unit 5 Definitions

The previous units were concerned with describing things. When we describe things we sometimes need to define them as well, especially in academic writing, so that it is perfectly clear what we mean. We may also need to give examples of what we define, and to classify. These will be covered in the following units.

**Stage 1
Simple Definitions**

1 If we look in a dictionary for the word 'school' we may find:

school an institution where children are educated

More formally in writing we would put:

A school is an institution where children are educated.

Look at these other examples:

A doctor is a person who gives medical treatment to people.
Aluminium is a metal which is produced from bauxite.

> **Note:**   *Who* is used for persons, *which* is used for inanimate objects and animals, *where* is used for places.

Complete the following sentences in the same way as the examples above.

a   A college _____ students receive higher or professional education.
b   A dentist _____ treats people's teeth.
c   Steel _____ is produced from iron and carbon. (We can also say that steel is an alloy.)
d   An elephant _____ lives in Africa and Asia.
e   A professor _____ works in a university.
f   A library _____ books are kept for borrowing or referring to.

2 Join the sentences on the left below with the correct ones from those on the right. Use an appropriate relative pronoun to create a relative clause.

e.g. Bronze is an alloy. It is produced from copper and tin.
Bronze is an alloy *which* is produced from copper and tin.

1 An engineer is a person	a It produces electricity.
2 A microscope is an instrument	b He studies the way in which industry and trade produce and use wealth.
3 A generator is a machine	c He treats the diseases of animals.
4 A botanist is a person	d It makes distant objects appear nearer and larger.
5 A square is a geometric figure	e He designs machines, buildings or public works.
6 A cucumber is a vegetable	f It gives information on subjects in alphabetical order.
7 An economist is a person	g He studies plants.
8 An encyclopaedia is a book	h It makes very small near objects appear larger.
	i It is long and round with a dark green skin and light green watery flesh.
	j It has four equal sides and four right angles.

3 So far, in the definitions we have looked at, the language construction has been:

> Thing to be defined + verb + general class word +
> *wh*-word + particular characteristics, e.g. *A botanist is a person who studies plants.*

Three types of mistakes may occur when a short definition is being written:

1 An example may be given rather than a definition. An example may, of course, follow a definition but it should not take its place.
2 The general class, or the particular characteristics, may be omitted from the definition. It will then be incomplete.
3 The word to be defined, or another form of it, may be used in the definition itself. Clearly, if the reader does not already understand the word, he/she will not understand the repeated use of it.

Study the following definitions. Each one contains one of the mistakes listed above. Analyse the type of mistake (1, 2, 3 above) that has been made. Write the number of the type of mistake in the column provided. The first one has been done as an example.

DEFINITION	Type of mistake
An ammeter is used to measure electric current.	2
a	A lecturer is a person who lectures.	
b	A dictionary is a book like the *Longman Dictionary of Contemporary English.*	
c	A degree is given by a university to a student who has passed the appropriate examinations.	

4 Now re-write the definitions above in a more satisfactory way. An example has been done for you.

An ammeter is an instrument which is used to measure electric current.

Stage 2
Academic Definitions

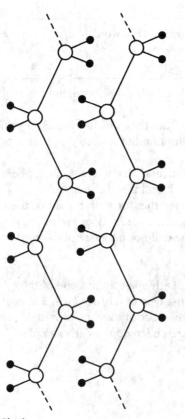

Plastics

1 Look at the following definition.

Plastics are compounds made with long chains of carbon atoms.

You will notice that the *wh*-word has been omitted. A definition written in this way uses a reduced relative clause. In full the definition would be:

Plastics are compounds *which are* made with long chains of carbon atoms.

Write out the following definitions in full, putting the *wh*-word in the correct place.

a Plastics are substances moulded into shape when they are heated.
b A mineral is a structurally homogeneous solid of definite chemical composition formed by the inorganic processes of nature.

Write out the following definitions omitting the *wh*-word so that a reduced relative clause is used.

c Rayons are man-made fibres which are produced from wood.
d A fossil is an inorganic trace which is buried by natural processes and subsequently permanently preserved.

2 Often subjects, particularly academic subjects, omit the *wh*-word in the following way:

Criminology *is the study of* crime (or illegal acts).
Psychiatry *is the study and treatment of* mental illness.
Politics *is the science of* government.
Botany *is the science of* the structure of plants.

Write out definitions of the subjects given below. Use the notes given next to each subject; write in the same style as above.

a Demography – study – population growth and its structure.
b Zoology – science – structure, forms and distribution of animals.
c Biology – science – physical life of animals and plants.

3 Academic subjects may be more cautiously defined, thus:

Geography *may be defined as the science of* the earth's surface.
Linguistics *may be defined as the science of* language.

Write out definitions of the following subjects in the same way as above.

a Sociology – science – nature and growth of society and social behaviour.
b Theology – study – religious beliefs and theories.
c Astronomy – science – sun, moon, stars and planets.

Write a definition of your subject in a similar way to the above.

**Stage 3
Extended Definitions**

1 It is possible for academic subjects to be defined more specifically. Normally, this can only be done if more information is given.

Look at the following example (*branch* has the meaning of *division*).

Psychology *may be defined as the branch of* biological science *which studies* the phenomena of conscious life and behaviour.

Write out definitions of the following subjects in the same way as above.

a Criminal psychology – psychology – investigates the psychology of crime and the criminal.
b Chemistry – science – deals with the composition and behaviour of substances.
c Social economics – economics – is concerned with the measurement, causes and consequences of social problems.

2 A definition may be extended in order to be more precise and/or to give more information about the subject. Look carefully at the following examples.

Sociology may be defined as the branch of science which studies the development and principles of social organisation. *It is concerned with* group behaviour as distinct from the behaviour of individuals in the group.

Econometrics may be defined as the branch of economics which applies mathematical and statistical techniques to economic problems. *It is concerned with* testing the validity of economic theories and providing the means of making quantitative predictions.

Now write a definition of your subject in a similar way to the above.

3 Use your dictionary to check definitions. Sometimes it is useful to compare definitions and explanations in two or three dictionaries: they are not always exactly the same, and they often give different examples.

Check the definitions of the following:

a   standard of living
b   household
c   durable goods
d   consumer
e   perishables

Note: These words are useful for Unit 11, Stage 3

Structure and Vocabulary Aid

A Frequently used verb forms for definitions

Present Simple (Active and Passive)

X | is . . .
means . . .
describes . . .
is defined as . . .
is used . . .

e.g.   A dialect is a variety of language.
It is spoken in one part of a country.

B Relative clauses

Relative clauses are often used to qualify or give extra information, e.g.

An X is someone who sells Y.
Y is something which is produced by Z.

C Useful verbs:

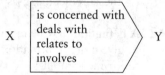

X | is concerned with
deals with
relates to
involves | Y

Unit 6   Exemplification

The last unit was concerned with definitions. It is often useful in definitions to give examples: this action is known as *exemplification* (or exemplifying).

Exemplifications are often introduced by *for example* or *e.g.*

> Linguistics may be defined as the science of language, *for example*, its structure, sound systems and meaning systems.

There are different ways of exemplifying, e.g.

> Geology may be defined as the science of the earth's history *as shown by* its crust, rocks, etc.

> Geography may be defined as the science of the earth's surface. It is concerned with a number of features, *particularly* physical, climate and products.

(Here *particularly* has the meaning 'more than some others'.)

Exemplification is commonly used throughout academic writing.

Stage 1
Words

1 Read the following carefully.

What is Language?

A language is a signalling system which operates with symbolic vocal sounds, and which is used by a group of people for the purposes of communication.

Let us look at this definition in more detail because it is
5 language, more than anything else, that distinguishes man from the rest of the animal world.

Other animals, it is true, communicate with one another by means of cries: for example, many birds utter warning calls at the approach of danger; apes utter different cries, such as
10 expressions of anger, fear and pleasure. But these various means of communication differ in important ways from human language. For instance, animals' cries are not articulate. This means, basically, that they lack structure. They lack, for example, the kind of structure given by the contrast
15 between vowels and consonants. They also lack the kind of structure that enables us to divide a human utterance into words.

We can change an utterance by replacing one word in it by another: a good illustration of this is a soldier who can say,
20 e.g. 'tanks approaching from the north', or he can change one word and say 'aircraft approaching from the north' or 'tanks approaching from the west'; but a bird has a single alarm cry, which means 'danger!'

This is why the number of signals that an animal can make
25 is very limited: the great tit is a case in point; it has about twenty different calls, whereas in human language the number of possible utterances is infinite. It also explains why animal cries are very general in meaning.

Read the passage again and draw a ⬚ box ⬚ around all the expressions which have the same meaning as *for example*. Notice how they are used and the punctuation that is used with them.

Now draw a line under all the examples, e.g.

⬚ such as ⬚ expressions of anger, fear and pleasure.

2 The following sentences are based upon the information contained in the passage above. Complete the sentences making use of each of the following words (use each one only once).

> illustration   for example   a case in point   an example
>   for instance   such as

a At the approach of danger many birds utter warning calls: this is _____ of animals communicating with each other.

b Cries, _____ those of anger, fear and pleasure, are uttered by apes.

c There are important differences between human language and animal communication: _____, animals' cries are not articulate.

d Animals' cries lack, _____, the kind of structure that enables us to divide a human utterance into words.

e A good _____ of changing an utterance by substituting one word for another is a soldier who can say 'tanks approaching from the north' or 'tanks approaching from the west'.

f The number of signals that an animal can make is very limited: the great tit is _____.

Stage 2
Sentences

1 Look at the following:

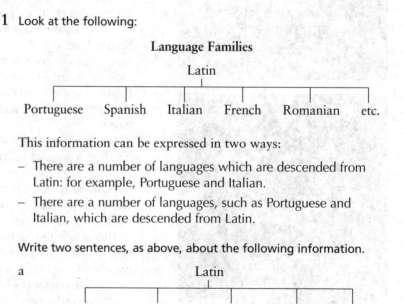

Language Families

Latin

Portuguese   Spanish   Italian   French   Romanian   etc.

This information can be expressed in two ways:

– There are a number of languages which are descended from Latin: for example, Portuguese and Italian.

– There are a number of languages, such as Portuguese and Italian, which are descended from Latin.

Write two sentences, as above, about the following information.

a   Latin

Romansch   Provençal   Catalan   Sardinian   etc.

b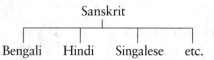

2 Read the following carefully, especially the part in italics.

There are now over two thousand different languages in the world; an examination of them shows that many of them belong to a group of related languages, and some of these groups are very large, constituting what we can call language families. *An example of such a family is the Semitic group of languages. Examples of members of the family are Arabic and Hebrew.*

Now write out the last two sentences substituting the following (not all the examples need to be listed):

a   Germanic – e.g. English, German, Dutch, Swedish, Danish, Norwegian.
b   Sino-Tibetan – e.g. Thai, Burmese, Chinese, Tibetan.

Stage 3
Paragraphs

1 Here are some notes on writing systems. Read them carefully.

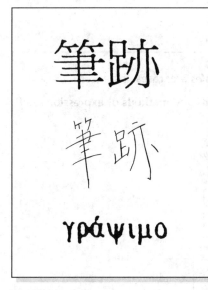

Top: Chinese
Centre: Japanese
Bottom: Greek

Writing Systems

Writing = method of human intercommunication by means of conventional visible marks.

Two main kinds of writing system:
1   ideographic (an ideogram or sign = one idea/word e.g. Chinese)
2   phonetic: a   syllabic (one sign = one syllable e.g. Amharic, Japanese kana)
                b   alphabetic (one sign = one sound e.g. Greek, Arabic)

Now write a paragraph on writing systems based on the information in the notes. Do not use notes in your writing, only complete sentences. Begin the paragraph with a definition of writing. Then continue with a description of the writing systems, beginning the sentence 'There are . . .' Remember to use sequence markers (connectives); practise using different expressions for *e.g.*

2 Write a definition of your own subject of study or research. Describe part of it, with examples.

Pyramid Discussion
Knowing a Foreign Language

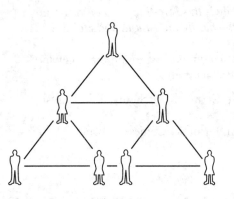

1 What are the three main advantages of knowing a foreign language? Select from the list below. The order of the choices is not important.

1　enables direct communication with a foreigner
2　gives access to a foreign literature
3　helps understanding of another culture
4　makes it easier to live/work in another country
5　helps if you want to study in another country
6　puts your own language and culture into perspective
7　helps you to understand the difficulties of people learning your language
8　personal satisfaction in mastering the skill
9　adds another dimension to education
10　enables you to make closer contact with other nationalities
11　helps understanding of other attitudes
12　makes it easier and cheaper to conduct business with another country
13　makes interpreters and translators unnecessary
14　enables you to understand information in another language
15　makes it easier to express your ideas to others

Finally, add some advantages of your own.

2 Write a brief explanation of the advantages of knowing a foreign language, with some examples.

Structure and Vocabulary Aid

A Alternatives to the word *examples* are: cases, instances.

B Other commonly used verb forms and methods of expression are:

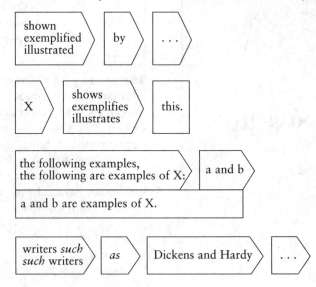

Unit 7   Classification

When we divide something into groups, classes, categories, etc. we are classifying those items. The classification is normally made according to a criterion or several criteria (standards or principles on which judgements are based).

Stage 1
Criteria

Top: Primary school
Centre: Comprehensive school
Bottom: Grammar school

1 Read the following carefully. Then complete the sentences below.

State Schools in England and Wales

The vast majority of children in Britain (87%) attend state (local authority) schools which provide compulsory education from the age of 5 to 16 years. These schools can be classified according to the age range of the pupils and the type of
5   education provided. Basically, there are two types of school, primary and secondary, although in some areas there are also middle schools. Primary schools cater for children aged 5–11, and secondary schools for ages 11–16 (and in some areas up to 18 years). Primary schools can be sub-divided into infant
10   schools (for ages 5–7) and junior schools (for ages 7–11).

Secondary schools are normally of one type for all abilities, viz. comprehensive schools. More than 90% of children in state schools attend this kind of school. In some areas middle schools exist as an extra level after primary school for children
15   aged 8 or 9 to 12 or 13. Pupils then transfer to comprehensive schools. In a very small number of areas, pupils may be grouped according to their ability and selected by means of an examination at the age of 11. In these areas, grammar schools cater for those who pass the exam. Those who fail go
20   to another secondary school.

When pupils reach the age of 16 there may be three choices open to them. Firstly, they may leave school. Secondly, they may stay on at school for two more years if it has a Sixth Form. Thirdly, they may transfer to a Sixth Form College, a Tertiary College or a Further Education College.

a   Schools _____ the pupils' ages and type of education.

b   There are _____ school: primary and secondary.

c   Primary schools _____ into infant and junior schools.

d   Secondary school pupils _____ their ability.

e   The criterion for classifying secondary schools is whether or not there is _____.

2 The sentences below summarise the information in the passage. However, they are in the wrong order. Put them in the correct order by writing numbers 1–7.

  a Most children go to comprehensive schools.

  b There may be three types of school: primary, middle and secondary.

  c At the age of sixteen, pupils may stay on at school, or leave and go to a college, or leave school altogether.

  d Exceptionally, children may take a selection exam at 11 years and go to a grammar school if they pass.

  e Most children go to state schools.

  f If children attend middle schools, they go on to comprehensive schools afterwards.

  g Primary schools comprise both infant and junior schools.

3 Look at Diagram 1. It shows a diagrammatic classification of state schools in England and Wales. If necessary read the text again and then complete Diagram 1, writing on the lines provided.

Diagram 1: State Schools in England and Wales

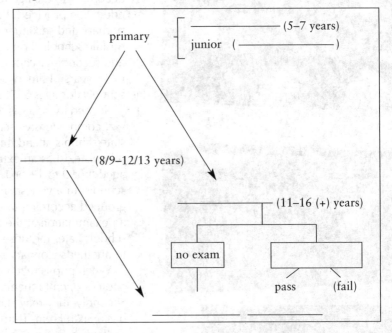

4 Without looking at the text again, write a brief description of the information contained in Diagram 1. Begin your description:

There are two types of school: primary and secondary. Primary schools can be sub-divided, according to age, into . . .

Note: If any help is needed with the language classification in this exercise, or the following ones, turn to the Structure and Vocabulary Aid at the end of this unit.

5 Draw a classification diagram of the education system in your country. When you have completed it, write a brief description of it.

Stage 2
Classifying

1 Read the following carefully. Then complete Diagram 2 ('The Classification of Birds') below.

The Classification of Birds

Birds are instantly recognisable creatures. Perhaps it is their ability to fly that causes this. Some people might consider that their shape was the most distinguishing feature. Everyone, however, agrees on the characteristics that a bird possesses:
5 two wings, feathers, two legs, a toothless bill or beak, warm blood, and it lays eggs.

The modern system of classifying birds is like a pyramid, with the base formed by 8514 different *species*. A convenient definition of species is: an interbreeding group of birds which
10 do not normally mate with other such groups.

The next division above the species is the *genus*, a group of species showing strong similarities. The scientific name of a bird gives the genus first, then the species. Thus, the scientific (Latin) name of the golden eagle is 'Aquila chrysaëtos' (eagle,
15 golden). When there are strong points of similarity between one genus and another, these related genera are grouped together and are said to belong to the same *family*. The names of the 215 families of birds always end in 'idae'. The golden eagle, for instance, is one of the 'Falconidae' (falcon family).

20 Families with broadly similar characteristics are grouped together into 27 *orders*, whose names end in 'iformes'. The golden eagle falls into the order of 'Falconiformes' (falcon-like birds). The largest order is 'Passeriformes' or perching birds. This contains 63 families, and more species than all the rest
25 put together. The feet are designed so that they can grip a perch, with three toes in front and one behind. In addition, all are known as song-birds. Two large families within this order are sparrows, with 155 species, and crows, with 100 species.

Finally, all of the orders make up the *class* 'Aves' (birds).
30 This system of classification has enabled scientists to differentiate 8514 species of birds. Placing a bird in the right family depends upon a number of features. Among them are external characteristics, such as the shape of the beak and feet, and the colour pattern of the feathers. However, at the
35 level of order, the next higher category, distinctions are based on such features as the structure of the skull, the arrangement of the muscles in the legs, and the condition of the young at the time of hatching.

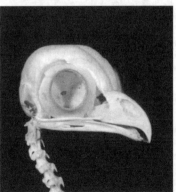

Top: Golden eagle
Centre: Sparrow
Bottom: Crow
Right: Skull of owl

Diagram 2: The Classification of Birds

Classification divisions or categories	Example of classification of Golden Eagle (in English) for each division	Number of the divisions
Order	Falcon-like	
	Golden Eagle	8514

2 From the information in the text:
  a give a definition of a bird.
  b give a definition of a species.
  c give two criteria that are used in assigning birds to the order of Passeriformes.
  d give two examples of families of birds from the order of Passeriformes.
  e list some of the general characteristics of families of birds, and then of orders of birds.

3 Write a brief general description of the classification of birds. Base your description upon the information contained in Diagram 2. Write in a similar way to the following classification of vegetables.

There are six main groups of vegetables, for example, legumes. Each group may be divided into members, such as beans, and each member may be sub-divided into types: Scarlet Runners are an example. Finally, each type may be further sub-divided into a number of varieties, e.g. Prizewinner.

Stage 3
Diagrams

1 Look carefully at Diagram 3. It is a tree diagram classification of drinks. What are the three criteria that are used in the classification?

2 Write a description of the classification of drinks based on the information in Diagram 3. Begin your description:
Drinks may be classified into two main groups: . . .

Diagram 3: A Classification of Drinks

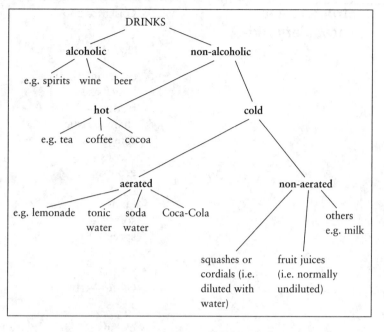

An aerated/carbonated/sparkling drink

3 Now draw a diagram for the subject, or part of it, that you are studying. Write a brief description of the classification diagram, making sure that it is clear what the criteria are. If a classification diagram is not appropriate for your subject, perhaps an organisational diagram (showing hierarchy etc.) would be possible.

Pyramid Discussion
The Purposes of Compulsory Education

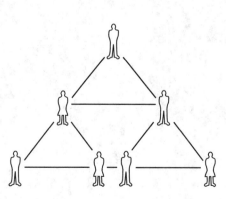

1 Which three purposes of compulsory education are the most important? Select from the list below. The order of the choices is not important. Finally, add a purpose of your own.

   1 to teach reading, writing and arithmetic ('the 3 Rs')
   2 to train for employment
   3 to create discipline
   4 to educate generally
   5 to develop character
   6 to teach sharing and co-operation with others
   7 to teach self-control
   8 to increase knowledge
   9 to help become a useful member of society
   10 to help to become self-aware
   11 to build a foundation for later studies or work
   12 to develop the mind
   13 to encourage independence in thinking
   14 to teach about the world around us
   15 to enable one to be an individual

2 Write a brief description of the criteria that can be or should be used for determining if education has been successful.

Structure and Vocabulary Aid

A Classification

Useful Nouns

criterion/criteria	breeds
basis/bases	orders
features	divisions
characteristics	families
categories	members
classes	sub-categories
groups	sub-classes
types	sub-groups
kinds	sub-orders
sorts	sub-divisions
species	

Useful Verbs

to . . .

classify	place in
categorise	distinguish (between)
group	differentiate (between/from)
divide into	sub-classify
arrange (in)	sub-categorise
put into	sub-group
fall into	sub-divide

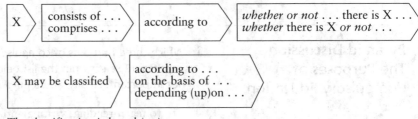

X ⟩ consists of . . . / comprises . . . ⟩ according to ⟩ *whether or not* . . . there is X . . . / *whether* there is X *or not* . . . ⟩

X may be classified ⟩ according to . . . / on the basis of . . . / depending (up)on . . . ⟩

The classification is based (up)on . . .

Note the possible sequence:

. . . may be divided . . . / . . . may be sub-divided . . . / . . . may be further sub-divided . . . ⟩

B Schools in England and Wales

State: non-fee-paying

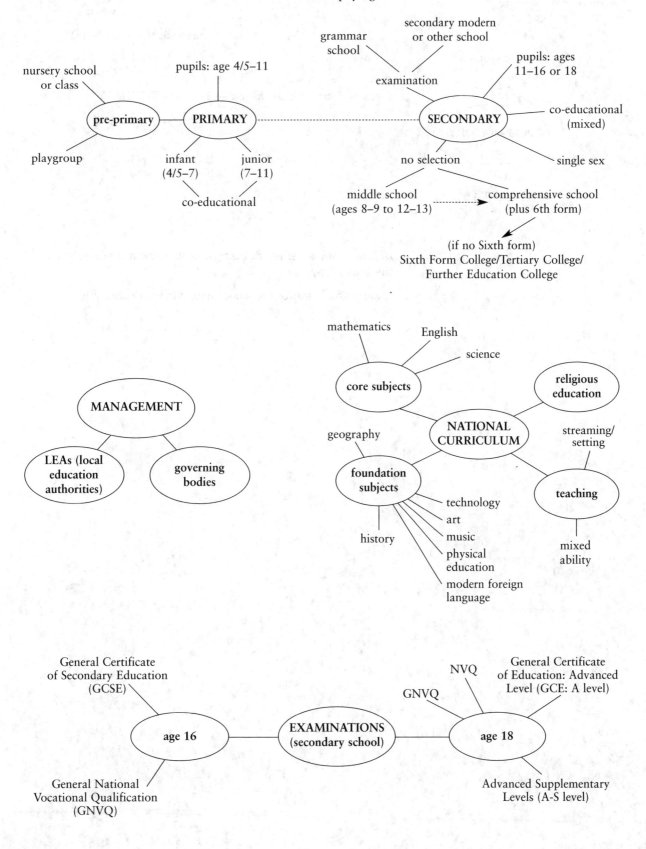

Independent: private, fee-paying

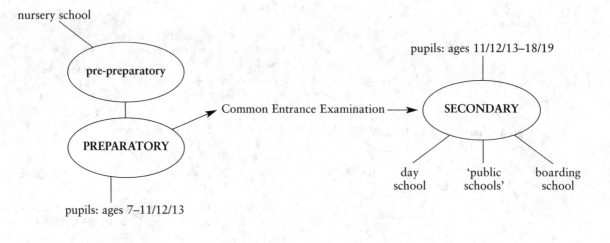

1 Are there any other words that you would find it useful to add to the above lists?

2 Make a similar list for the school system in your country.

Unit 8   Comparison and Contrast

In most academic subjects, and in life generally, we often need to *compare* and *contrast* things. Similarities and differences are often noted when classifying (see the previous unit). The language of comparison and contrast is frequently needed when studying tables and other statistical information. The language forms used in this unit are to be found in Appendix 1, Section 3.

**Stage 1
Comparison**

1 Look at Tables 1 and 2 and complete these sentences. If necessary, look at Appendix 1, Section 3, Comparisons. Put one or more words in each space.

Table 1

a   The Nile is _____ the Mississippi-Missouri.
b   The Amazon is _____ long _____ the Nile.
c   The Nile is _____ river in the world.
d   The Mississippi-Missouri is _____ the Amazon.
e   The Yangtse is _____ river in China.

Table 2

f   In Beijing, January is a _____ month _____ December.
g   July is a _____ month _____ June.
h   There is _____ rain in May _____ in March.
i   July has the _____ rain; in other words, July is _____ month.
j   August is _____ warm _____ July.
k   December and January are _____ months.
l   The rainfall in February is _____ in March.
m   April is _____ wet _____ October.
n   The rainfall in November is _____ in May.
o   July is the _____ month, and also _____ month.

Satellite view of the River Nile

Table 1: The Longest Rivers in the World

1	The Nile (Africa)—4,160 miles (6,695 kilometres)
2	The Amazon (South America)—4,080 miles (6,570 kilometres)
3	The Mississippi-Missouri (North America)—3,740 miles (6,020 kilometres)
4	The Yangtse (Asia: China)—3,430 miles (5,520 kilometres)

Table 2: Temperatures and Rainfall in Beijing, China

Month	J	F	M	A	M	J	J	A	S	O	N	D
Temperature (°C)	−4.7	−1.5	5.0	13.7	19.9	24.5	26.0	24.7	19.8	12.5	3.6	−2.6
Rainfall (cm)	0.2	0.5	0.5	1.5	3.6	7.6	23.9	16.0	6.6	1.5	0.8	0.2

Note: The first month is January (J), the last is December (D).

Everest

2 Look at Table 3. Write at least three sentences comparing the mountains, which are all in the Himalayas,

Table 3: The Highest Mountains in the World

> 1 Everest (Nepal/Tibet) – 29,028 feet (8,848 metres)
>
> 2 K2 (Pakistan/India) – 28,250 feet (8,611 metres)
>
> 3 Kangchenjunga (Nepal/Sikkim) – 28,168 feet (8,586 metres)
>
> 4 Lhotse (Nepal/Tibet) – 27,923 feet (8,511 metres)
>
> 5 Makalu (Nepal/Tibet) – 27,805 feet (8,475 metres)
>
> 6 Dhaulagiri (Nepal) – 26,795 feet (8,167 metres)

3 Turn back to Unit 2 Stage 2. Look at the information in the table about Manchester University students. Write several sentences comparing the information: e.g. More students write essays than any other type of writing.

Stage 2
Extended Comparison

1 Read the following carefully.

Several years ago, some research was conducted at Manchester University into the amount of time that overseas postgraduate students spent listening to spoken English and speaking English. Sixty students co-operated by completing
5 questionnaires.

It was found that an average of $22\frac{3}{4}$ hours per week were spent listening to English and only $6\frac{1}{4}$ hours speaking English to English people. An analysis of the time spent listening to English showed that lectures accounted for 5 hours and
10 seminars 2 hours. An estimated $2\frac{1}{2}$ hours were spent in serious discussion while 2 hours were devoted to everyday small-talk. Watching television accounted for $5\frac{1}{4}$ hours and listening to the radio $4\frac{1}{2}$ hours. Going to the cinema or theatre only accounted for an average of $\frac{3}{4}$ hour per week.

The following sentences are based upon the information contained in the text above. Complete the sentences by choosing from the list of words and phrases below: use each word once only. Make sure that you keep the same meaning in the sentences as in the text.

Choose from these words: *biggest; as much . . . as; more . . . than* (twice); *least; most; not so many . . . as; as many . . . as; the same . . . as; greater . . . than.*

a The students spent considerably _____ time listening to English _____ speaking it.

b A _____ amount of time was spent in lectures _____ in seminars.

c Nearly _____ hours were spent listening to the radio _____ watching television.

d The _____ popular way of listening to English
was by watching TV.

e _____ number of hours was spent in everyday
small-talk _____ in taking part in seminars.

f The _____ popular way of listening to English
was by going to the cinema.

g _____ hours were spent in serious discussion
_____ in watching television.

h Nearly _____ time was spent in watching
television _____ in speaking English.

i _____ time was spent in serious discussion
_____ in everyday small-talk.

j The _____ surprise in the survey was the small
number of hours spent speaking English to English people.

2 You have just received a letter from a friend, or acquaintance,
asking for some information about English dictionaries and asking
you to recommend a suitable one to help him/her learn English.
Look at Table 4: English Learners' Dictionaries, then on the basis of
that information write a letter recommending one of the
dictionaries. Give reasons for your choice. Look at the Structure and
Vocabulary Aid at the end of this unit and at the Notes in the Key if
you need some help with the letter.

Table 4: English Learners' Dictionaries

Feature / Dictionary	Words and phrases	Examples	Pages	Words illustrated	Appendices	Level
Longman Dictionary of Contemporary English	80,000	62,700	1,690	2,300	8	upper intermediate – advanced
Longman Active Study Dictionary	45,000	25,000	807	16 pages	5	intermediate
Oxford Advanced Learner's Dictionary	63,000	90,000	1,428	1,700	10	upper intermediate – advanced
Oxford Student's Dictionary	42,000	23,500	748	–	4	intermediate
Cambridge International Dictionary of English	100,000	110,000	1,792	2,000	2	intermediate plus
Collins COBUILD English Dictionary	75,000	100,000	1,951	–	–	intermediate – advanced

Pyramid Discussion
Reasons for Using a Dictionary

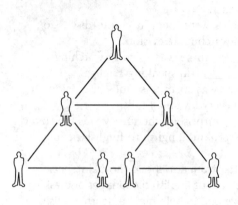

1 What are the three main reasons for using a dictionary? Select from the list below. The order of the choices is not important.

1 to find meanings
2 to find synonyms
3 to check spellings
4 for word pronunciation and stress
5 to see the differences between confused words
6 for information about grammar
7 for information about style (e.g. formal, slang)
8 for usage and examples
9 for information about abbreviations, names etc. (in the appendices)
10 to check idioms, phrases, proverbs
11 to extend knowledge of vocabulary
12 for accurate information about words

Finally, add any other reasons not given here.

2 Write a brief comparison of the main reasons for using a dictionary.

Stage 3
Similarities and Differences

1 **Similarities**

There are a number of language constructions that express similarity apart from those listed in Appendix 1, Section 3.

Look at the following examples based on Table 5.
a *Both* Belgium *and* Canada have a small agricultural population.
b Belgium and Canada are *similar* (or *alike*) *in that* they both have a small agricultural population.
c Belgium, *like* Canada, has a small agricultural population.
d Canada *is similar to* Nepal *in* its percentage of forest area.
e Canada *is similar to* Nepal *in that* it has a large forest area.

> **Note:** Still more sentences may be composed by using the connectives listed in Appendix 2: Connectives (section 1A: Addition), e.g. *Belgium has a small agricultural population; so, too, does Canada.*

Now write sentences similar to those above, basing your information on Table 5.

Table 5: Various Countries

Information ＼ Country	Belgium	Canada	Egypt	Ireland	Nepal
Population	10,140,000	29,972,000	64,100,000	3,589,000	21,953,000
Area: sq. km.	32,800	9,221,000	995,000	68,900	137,000
Density: per sq. km.	323	3	52	53	136
Forest area	21%	39%	0	4.5%	39%
Arable land (for crops)	23.5%	5%	2%	13.5%	17%
Agricultural population	2%	3%	39%	12%	91%
Main languages	Dutch/ Flemish, French	English, French	Arabic, French	English, Irish	Nepali, Maithili
Main religions	Christianity	Christianity	Islam	Christianity	Hinduism, Buddhism

2 **Differences**

For a number of ways of expressing difference, see Appendix 1, Section 3 and Appendix 2, Section 3.

Look at the following examples based on Table 5.
a Ireland and Belgium are *dissimilar in that* Ireland has a *much* small*er* population *than* Belgium.
b *With regard to* population, Egypt is (much) big*ger than* Canada.
c The main religion in Belgium is Christianity, *whereas* in Egypt it is Islam.
d Belgium has *the* large*st* percentage arable land area; *however*, it has *the* small*est* percentage agricultural population.
e *Although* Belgium has *the* large*st* percentage arable land area, it has *the* small*est* percentage agricultural population.
f *On the one hand*, Canada has *the* large*st* population; *on the other hand*, it has *the* low*est* density of population.

Now write some sentences similar to those above, basing your information on Table 5.

3 Turn to Unit 3, Stage 2. Look at the table of information about Australia beneath the map. Write a paragraph to compare and contrast Australia with Canada in terms of area, population, density, arable land area and forest area.

4 Compare and contrast your country with one of the countries in Table 5. It is not necessary to refer to all the items. If you do not know some of the details for your country, give a rough estimation; but try to find out by looking in appropriate reference books. If necessary, look at the Structure and Vocabulary Aid in this unit and in Unit 3 to help you.

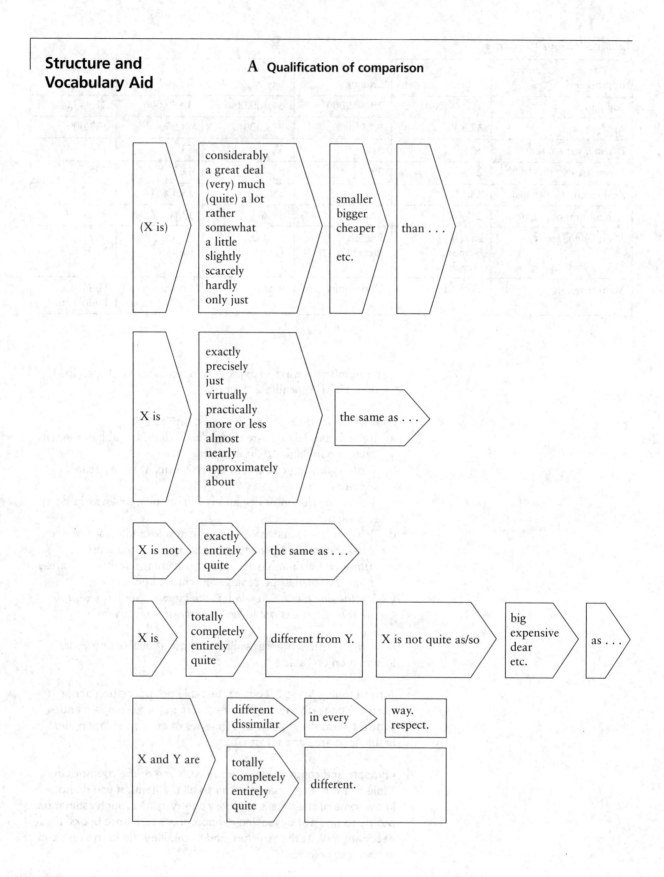

(X is) — considerably / a great deal / (very) much / (quite) a lot / rather / somewhat / a little / slightly / scarcely / hardly / only just — smaller / bigger / cheaper / etc. — than . . .

X is — exactly / precisely / just / virtually / practically / more or less / almost / nearly / approximately / about — the same as . . .

X is not — exactly / entirely / quite — the same as . . .

X is — totally / completely / entirely / quite — different from Y. | X is not quite as/so — big / expensive / dear / etc. — as . . .

X and Y are — different / dissimilar — in every — way. / respect.

X and Y are — totally / completely / entirely / quite — different.

B Cardinal numbers

When writing figures involving thousands, a space is used to separate the thousands if there are 5 or more digits:
e.g. 10 000   100 000   1 000 000   but 1000
Alternatively a comma may be used to separate the thousands:
e.g. 1,000   10,000   100,000   1,000,000

A point is used in writing decimal fractions: e.g. 1293.75

C Ordinal numbers

Ordinal numbers are often written in abbreviated form:
1st – first
2nd – second
3rd – third
4th – fourth
5th – fifth

'th' is used after all numbers except those ending in 1, 2, or 3.

D Percentages (%)

Figures	Language
10%	ten per cent
1.5%	one point five per cent or one and a half per cent
0.5%	(nought) point five per cent or half a per cent

Note: percentage = proportion
absolute number = total number

Unit 9   Cause and Effect

In academic writing, events and actions are frequently linked with their cause and effect. Look at the following diagram, which summarises this relationship.

back in time or sequence		forward in time or sequence
cause	event	effect
reason	situation	consequence
	action	result
	idea	solution
	problem	

There are a large number of ways to express the relationship shown in the diagram above. You will need to look at Appendix 2, Connectives (Section 1E: Result) and especially the Structure and Vocabulary Aid at the end of this unit before doing the exercises.

Now look at these examples of the cause and effect relationship.

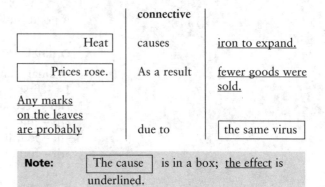

	connective	
Heat	causes	iron to expand.
Prices rose.	As a result	fewer goods were sold.
Any marks on the leaves are probably	due to	the same virus

Note: ⬛ The cause ⬛ is in a box; <u>the effect</u> is underlined.

Sometimes the cause will be named before the effect; sometimes the effect will be named first. e.g.

1)   **X** causes   **Y** (active verb)
         ↑   ↑
      cause   effect

2)   **Y** is caused by   **X** (passive verb)
        ↑   ↑
      effect   cause

Stage 1
Connectives and Markers

1 The parts of the sentences below have been mixed up. Join the six parts on the left with the correct parts from the nine on the right.

1	There is acid in that bottle: *therefore* . . .	a	the road was icy.
2	The *effect* of the fluctuation in temperature . . .	b	he was unsuccessful.
3	Bad labour relations *caused* . . .	c	prolonged illness.
4	The accident occurred *because of* . . .	d	it must be handled very carefully.
5	He passed his examination *because* . . .	e	careful storage.
6	Delayed treatment often *results in* . . .	f	the icy road conditions.
		g	the strike.
		h	he worked hard.
		i	was to kill the laboratory specimens.

2 Making use of the information in the correct answers from the previous exercise, complete the following sentences. Inside the box write the appropriate connective or verb marker (see the Structure and Vocabulary Aid). The first one has been done as an example.

e.g. Icy road conditions ☐ caused ☐ ___the accident___ .

a ☐ ☐ he worked hard _____ .

b Prolonged illness is often ☐ _____ .

c The strike was ☐ _____ .

d The laboratory specimens were killed ☐ _____ .

e That bottle must be handled very carefully ☐ _____ .

Stage 2
Identifying Relationships

Top: Glacier
Left: Silver birch trees
Above: Spruce trees

1 Read the following carefully.

Climate

For the last hundred years the climate has been growing much warmer. This has had a number of different effects. Since the beginning of the twentieth century, glaciers have been melting very rapidly. For example, the Muir Glacier in Alaska has
5 retreated two miles in ten years. Secondly, rising temperatures have been causing the snowline to retreat on mountains all over the world. In Peru, for example, it has risen as much as 2700 feet in 60 years.

As a result of this, vegetation has also been changing. In
10 Canada, the agricultural cropline has shifted 50 to 100 miles northward. In the same way cool-climate trees like birches and spruce have been dying over large areas of Eastern Canada. In Sweden the treeline has moved up the mountains by as much as 65 feet since 1930.
15 The distribution of wildlife has also been affected, many European animals moving northwards into Scandinavia. Since 1918, 25 new species of birds have been seen in Greenland, and in the United States birds have moved their nests to the north.
20 Finally, the sea has been rising at a rapidly increasing rate, largely due, as was mentioned above, to the melting of glaciers. In the last 18 years it has risen by about six inches, which is about four times the average rate of rise over the last 9000 years.

Now look at the following cause and effect table. From the text above copy into the table where necessary the causes and effects mentioned; also write in the central column, the appropriate connective or marker of the cause/effect relationship. Where an example (e.g.) is asked for, only write the first one if more than one is given in the text. The first section has been done as an example.

Table 1: *Climate*

Cause	Connective or Marker	Effect
The climate has been growing much warmer	(different) effects	1 glaciers have been melting very rapidly, e.g. the Muir Glacier in Alaska has retreated 2 miles in 10 years
		2 e.g.
		3 e.g.
		4 e.g.
		5 e.g.

2 Look at Table 2 carefully. Complete the description that follows of the information it contains. In the spaces write a suitable cause-effect connective.

Table 2: *Accidents in a large British city (1996)*

	Main accident causes	number of accidents 1996	percentage rise (+)/fall (−) compared with 1995
1	Drivers turning right without due care	593	+12%
2	Pedestrians crossing roads carelessly	402	+ 7%
3	Drivers failing to give a signal	231	− 3%
4	Drivers losing control of vehicles	312	+40%
5	Drivers improperly overtaking other vehicles	173	−10%
6	Drivers misjudging distances	96	−20%

Firstly, turning right without due care (1) _____ 593 accidents in 1996. Secondly, (2) _____ pedestrians crossed roads carelessly, 402 accidents occurred. Next, although there was a 3% decrease in drivers failing to give a signal, nevertheless there were still 231 accidents (3) _____ this. In 1996, 40% more drivers than in 1995 lost control of vehicles. (4) _____ there were

312 accidents. In fifth place came drivers improperly overtaking other vehicles: these (5) _____ 173 accidents. Finally, there was a 20% fall in drivers misjudging distances; however, they were still the (6) _____ 96 accidents.

3 Now write a description of Table 3 in a similar way to the previous exercise. Practise using different connectives but take care to use the correct construction.

Table 3: Accidents in a large British city (1998)

Main accident causes		number of accidents 1998	percentage rise (+)/fall (−) compared with 1997
1	Drivers travelling too close to other vehicles	347	+ 7%
2	Drivers driving under the influence of alcohol	304	+10%
3	Drivers reversing negligently	169	− 8%
4	Pedestrians crossing roads in dangerous places	113	− 5%
5	Drivers travelling too quickly in bad weather conditions	190	+12%

Stage 3
Main Causes and Effects

1 Look at this diagram relating to poverty. Write one or two paragraphs describing some of the causes and effects of poverty in Britain or another industrialised country that you know of. In your description include a definition of poverty.

POVERTY
(the state of being very poor)

SOME CAUSES
low wages
unemployment
death of the wage-earner
large families
illness
old age
alcohol
gambling
lack of education
government policies
inflation
war
natural disasters
(drought, famine, flood,
earthquake)

SOME EFFECTS
inadequate, insufficient
or no –
    accommodation
    food
    clothing
    heating
    opportunities
    amenities
    possessions or
    comforts

> **Note:** Causes can have multiple effects, and there can be a circular relationship between cause and effect e.g. unemployment → very little money → few opportunities or amenities → alcohol → illness . . . ?

2 Describe poverty in your country – its main causes and effects. (Who are the poor? Where do they live? Why are they poor? What is the effect on them?)

3 Briefly describe the cause-effect relationship of part of your own specialist subject or of some aspect of studies which you are familiar with.

Structure and Vocabulary Aid

Cause-effect relationships

Look carefully at the connectives or markers of cause-effect relationships shown below. Notice particularly how they are used in a sentence construction. The shaded boxes refer to causes.

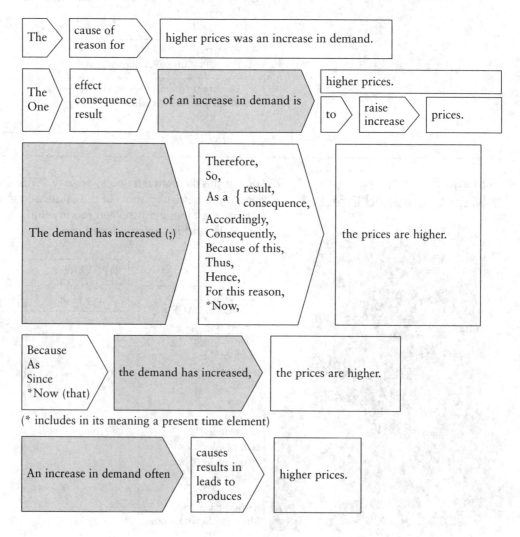

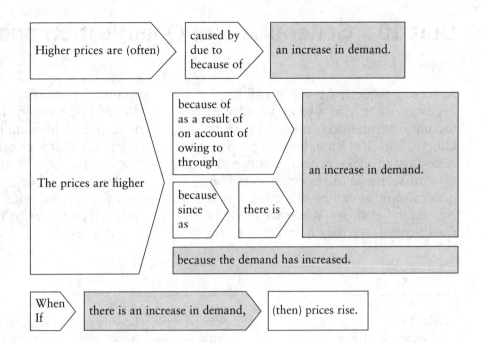

Higher prices are (often) | caused by / due to / because of | an increase in demand.

The prices are higher | because of / as a result of / on account of / owing to / through | an increase in demand.

because / since / as | there is | an increase in demand.

because the demand has increased.

When / If | there is an increase in demand, | (then) prices rise.

Unit 10   Generalisation, Qualification and Caution

In some academic writing it will be necessary simply to give and describe factual information (similar to that in Units 2 and 3). Often, however, it is necessary to make general comments or to generalise about the information. The generalisations can be made more precise by qualifying them. When we make a qualification we may be giving our own opinion or interpreting the information: this will be examined in more detail in the next unit. Additionally, in academic writing, we often need to be careful about any claims that we make. Such 'cautious' language is looked at in Stage 3. For exercises throughout this unit it will be necessary to refer to the Structure and Vocabulary Aid.

Stage 1
Generalisation

1   Compare the following two paragraphs. The first is a straightforward description of factual information. In the second, the figures have been changed to generalisations. Underline the changes in the second paragraph.

A Survey of Unemployment (1)

A recent survey of people out of work analysed the type of worker who is unemployed. Out of the one million registered as unemployed, one in five were women. 60% of men who were unemployed were to be found in services and engineering. There was a one in eight chance of being unemployed in the construction industry. One in twenty were unemployed in industries such as metal goods and textiles.

A Survey of Unemployment (2)

A recent survey of people out of work analysed the type of worker who is unemployed. Out of all those registered as unemployed a minority were women. The majority of men who were unemployed were to be found in services and engineering. There was also a likelihood of being unemployed in the construction industry. There was a little unemployment in industries such as metal goods and textiles.

2   Read the paragraphs below. A number of generalisations have been made which involve qualifying statements. With the help of the Structure and Vocabulary Aid, identify the qualifications of quantity, frequency and probability in these paragraphs and in 'A Survey of Unemployment (2)' above, and write them in the table below. The first ones have been done as examples.

If somebody was unemployed from engineering, mining or chemicals, he could usually find another job. However, an unemployed person from agriculture or construction seldom found a job again. Job chances were generally much better for manual workers than for office workers.

Most of the unemployed had been without jobs for more than two months. A number had been unemployed for more than a year. Undoubtedly the longer a person is out of work, the more likely it is that he will not find another job. In addition, job prospects are definitely worse for older workers.

Quantity	Frequency	Probability
all	usually	possible

Stage 2
Qualification

1 Look at the following information which relates to a British university. It shows some of the forms that overseas students completed during their first few weeks in Britain last year. Write a paragraph describing the information in the table. Use quantity qualifications instead of percentage figures. Begin 'Last year all overseas students completed University Registration forms . . .'

%	Form
100	University Registration
95	University Library Membership Application
80	National Health Service Registration
56	International Student Identity Card Application
35	Accommodation Office Application
3	Magazine Subscription

2 Use the information in the table to make generalised predictive statements about students coming to the university next year and form-filling. Make use of probability expressions in order to do this, as in the example:

It is certain that (all) students will need to complete a University Registration form.

3 Recently science students were asked if they had difficulty in obtaining their course books from libraries. The diagram indicates their responses.

Changing the percentage figures to quantity qualifications, describe the information, e.g.

A few students were never able to obtain their course books from libraries.

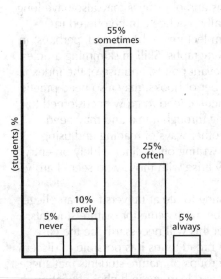

Stage 3
Caution

A feature of written academic English is the need to be careful or cautious. Thus, unless there is evidence which indicates 100% certainty, statements or conclusions are normally qualified in some way to make them less definite (therefore words like *all*, *always*, *never*, are usually avoided). The purpose is to be accurate and not to make false claims, or claims that may be challenged by others. In other words, allowance should be made for other possible points of view. There are two basic ways of doing this: a) through words from the lists in the Scale of Qualification, especially the Probability list and sometimes the Frequency list; and b) through the Impersonal verb phrases that do not declare the writer's own attitude, and also the use of some nouns and adverbs (see Structure and Vocabulary Aid).

1 In the sentences below there are a number of examples of cautious language. Underline the appropriate words or write a list giving the line numbers. If necessary, refer to the Structure and Vocabulary Aid.

Adjusting to Higher Education

New students may refer to feelings of bewilderment because of the differences in size between school and a large university. The sheer variety of possible activities can be confusing. Students who have chosen to cater for themselves
5 may, at first, have difficulty in finding time for shopping and housekeeping. To these domestic problems may be added financial difficulties when grants fail to arrive, often in the case of foreign students who have no family at hand to assist them.
10   Discussion with students in various university departments suggests that a quite common complaint is that they do not know what their teachers expect of them. Failure to specify and to communicate aims and objectives may also have long-term consequences. Initially practice can be offered in
15 reading, taking notes from lectures or books and, perhaps, in writing brief reports or paragraphs. Skill in skimming articles to select important or relevant points, and use of the index to look up a topic in a number of books, may also need practice. Science students, in particular, tend to grow accustomed to
20 careful, sequential reading through a text and may need reminding that there are other ways of reading and using books. Students' skills in writing often differ widely on entry. Problems most frequently arise with those who seem hardly literate initially.
25   The problems of adjusting to life at university or a college of higher education can be more acute for mature students, but it does not follow that this will necessarily be the case. Nonetheless, speaking in broad terms it is possible to discern some similarities within groups of mature students that suggest
30 implications for teaching and learning in higher education. It appears, for example, from various studies, that there are three main reasons why adults take up full-time study: (1) to make a

change in their career; (2) to obtain a job qualification – for such reasons as job promotion; (3) to seek personal and
35 intellectual development.

The difficulties facing adult learners can, for convenience, be categorised into three kinds – social, psychological and physiological. But for others such problems do not seem to arise.

(Based on extracts from *Teaching and Learning in Higher Education* by Ruth Beard and James Hartley.)

2 Look carefully at the table below. It lists the language difficulties of overseas students studying in Britain. It compares their problems on arrival with their problems six months later.

English language problems of overseas students in Britain

Language problems	Students: percentage	
	on arrival	6 months later
understanding spoken English	66%	28%
speaking	52%	42%
writing	15%	32%
reading	3%	2%

Note: the percentage figures total more than 100% because some students listed more than one problem.

Now read the paragraph below which comments on some of the information. Complete the final sentence by adding some possible reasons.

On arrival in Britain the biggest language problem for overseas students is understanding spoken English. It would seem that the main reasons for this are difficulties in understanding local accents and the speed of speaking of British people. Six months later the problem has declined into third place. It is generally agreed that the main reasons for this are . . .

3 Write three more paragraphs to describe the remainder of the information in the table above. Make use of the Impersonal verb phrases in the Structure and Vocabulary Aid to indicate that cautious conclusions are being reached.

Some possible reasons to account for the difficulties (not the improvements) are: local accent, speed of speaking, lack of fluency, limited vocabulary, lack of practice, poor teaching, lack of opportunity, poor pronunciation, slow reading speed, literal translation, poor grammar.

4 Briefly describe the main English language difficulties of students from your country.

Structure and Vocabulary Aid

A Scale of qualification

percentage guide	QUANTITY	FREQUENCY	PROBABILITY		
			Adverbs	Adjectives	Verbs
100%	all/every/each most a majority (of) many/much a lot (of) enough some a number (of) several a minority (of) a few/a little few/little	always usual(ly) normal(ly) general(ly) on the whole regular(ly) often frequent(ly) sometimes occasional(ly) rare(ly) seldom hardly ever	certainly definitely undoubtedly clearly presumably probably conceivably possibly perhaps maybe uncertainly	certain definite undoubted clear (un)likely probable possible uncertain	will is/are must/have to should would ought to may might can could
0%	no/none/not any	never			will is/are } + not can could

If you are uncertain if a word is quantity or frequency you can normally check by seeing if it can be used to answer the following questions:

Quantity: How many? How much?
Frequency: How often?

Some of the probability qualifications can be further qualified, e.g.

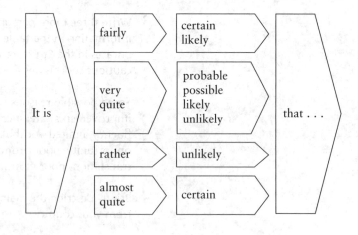

Sometimes generalisations may be introduced or qualified in the following way:

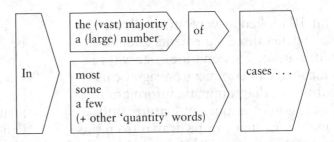

In ⟩ the (vast) majority / a (large) number ⟩ of ⟩ cases . . .

most / some / a few / (+ other 'quantity' words)

B Caution: Impersonal verb phrases

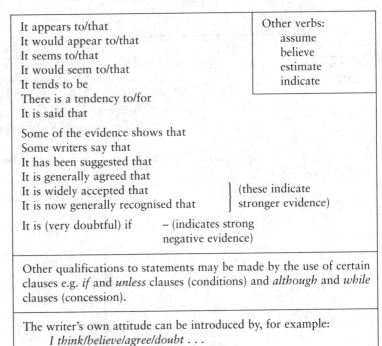

	Other verbs:
It appears to/that	assume
It would appear to/that	believe
It seems to/that	estimate
It would seem to/that	indicate
It tends to be	
There is a tendency to/for	
It is said that	

Some of the evidence shows that
Some writers say that
It has been suggested that
It is generally agreed that
It is widely accepted that } (these indicate
It is now generally recognised that   stronger evidence)

It is (very doubtful) if   – (indicates strong negative evidence)

Other qualifications to statements may be made by the use of certain clauses e.g. *if* and *unless* clauses (conditions) and *although* and *while* clauses (concession).

The writer's own attitude can be introduced by, for example:
      I think/believe/agree/doubt . . .
(See Unit 12: Structure and Vocabulary Aid)

An example of using a 'cautious verb':

Industrialisation *tends to* be viewed as a superior way of life.

C Caution: Some other adverbs and nouns

Adverbs	Nouns
apparently	assumption
approximately	claim
hardly	estimate
practically	evidence
presumably	possibility
relatively	presumption
scarcely	chance
seemingly	likelihood
slightly	
virtually	

Unit 11   Interpretation of Data

Unit 10 looked at ways in which we can make generalised statements about information. This unit looks at ways in which we can comment on significant features in diagrammatic information. Discussion of important features and conclusions that can be drawn from this information is covered in Units 12 and 13.

For exercises throughout this unit it will be necessary to refer to the Structure and Vocabulary Aid at the end of the unit. Comparisons and contrasts will frequently be made: you may need to refer to the Structure and Vocabulary Aid at the end of Unit 8, and to Appendix 1, Section 3.

Stage1
Charts

Although the information contained in charts and diagrams is normally clear, it usually requires some written comment. Not all the information should be described. It is usual to introduce the information with a general comment and then describe or comment on the most significant or important information.

1   Look at the following chart carefully and then read the text below.

Chart 1: Distribution of the world's population by continent

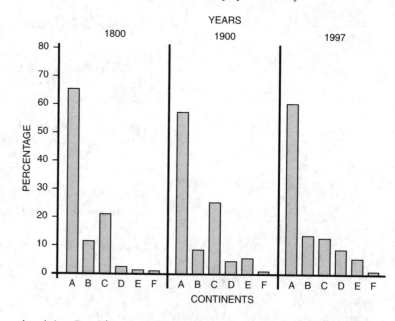

A = Asia   B = Africa   C = Europe   D = Latin America and Caribbean
E = North America   F = Oceania

Note:	Oceania – sometimes called Australasia – comprises Australia, New Zealand, Papua New Guinea and South Pacific islands

Introduction

Chart 1 (a bar chart or histogram) shows the distribution of the world's population by continent. The vertical axis shows the percentage of world population and the horizontal axis compares the six continents listed, divided into a comparison of three years: 1800, 1900 and 1997.

Comment

As can be seen from the chart, by far the largest percentage of the world's population lived in Asia compared with any other continent in 1800. In fact, Asia accounted for as much as 65% of the world's population. On the other hand, North America and Oceania together accounted for only 1% of the total.

Note:	1	*in fact* elaborates or expands the previous piece of information;
	2	*by far the largest*, *as much as* and *only* draw attention to significant items.

Comment on the percentage of the world's population living in Europe in 1900 using the information in Chart 1. Write in a similar way to the comment above, drawing attention to what is significant. See Notes on the Exercises at the back of the book for precise figures.

2 Comment generally on the information in Chart 1, comparing some continents and some years.

**Stage 2
Graphs**

1 The graph below shows the population of the UK at intervals of ten years. The first official census of population was taken in 1801. They have been taken every ten years since (except 1941 because of war). Comment on the information in the graph. Before you write, look at the Structure and Vocabulary Aid at the end of this unit and the Notes on the Exercises at the back of the book.

Graph 1: Population of the UK

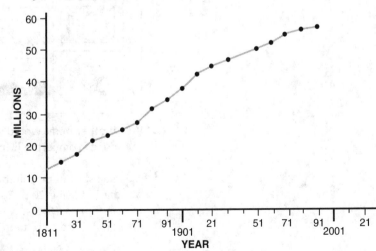

2 Estimate the UK population for the year 2021. Base your prediction on the trend shown in the graph.

3 Compare the population of your country and its trend with that of the UK.

Stage 3
Diagrams and Tables

1 One way to measure the improvement in the standard of living of a country, over a period of time, is to compare the percentage of people who own, or have access to, certain products that improve the way of life (e.g. make life easier, more comfortable, more enjoyable).

Comment on the significant items and trend(s) shown in the following diagram for the products listed for Britain – cars, central heating, washing machines, refrigerators (or fridges) and fridge-freezers, televisions and telephones.
(Can you give a satisfactory definition of: *standard of living*; *household*; *durable goods*?)

Diagram 1: Percentage of households with certain durable goods

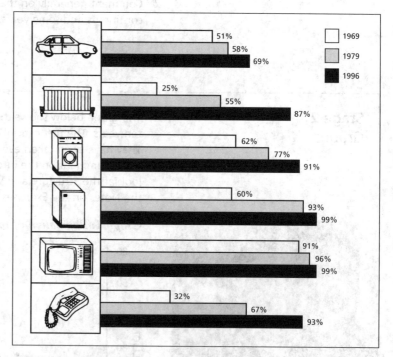

2 Which other items would you include in the list for Britain for the purpose of comparing living standards over a period of time?

3 Make a list of items suitable for your country to compare the standard of living 20 or 30 years ago with today. It is not necessary to give figures. Discuss with other students your choice of items. What differences are there? Why?

4 The following diagram (often called a pie chart) gives information about family spending in Britain. Look at the information and then write generalised comments that draw attention to the most significant items.

Diagram 2: Average weekly expenditure per family in Britain (1996)

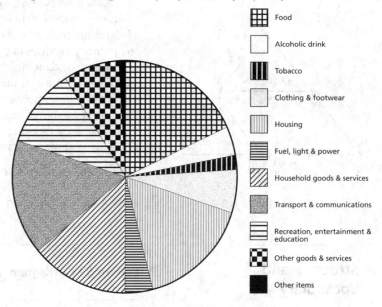

5 Draw a similar diagram of family spending for your own country, or for your family (exact figures are not needed). Briefly comment on the most significant items.

6 Comment on the trend(s) shown in the following table of family expenditure in Britain. Notice that the data for 1996 are shown in the pie chart above.

Table 1: Average family expenditure in Britain (%)

ITEM	1967	1977	1996
Food	21	19	18
Alcoholic drink	7	7	4
Tobacco	6	4	2
Clothing and footwear	9	8	6
Housing	12	14	16
Fuel, light and power	5	5	4
Household goods and services	10	7	14
Transport and communications	9	14	16
Recreation, entertainment and education	7	9	11
Other goods and services	14	12	8
Other items	–	1	1

Pyramid Discussion
Worthwhile Leisure Activities

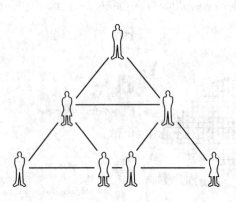

1 Which are the three most worthwhile leisure activities? Select from the list below. The order of the choices is not important.

1 watching TV and video
2 listening to music
3 reading books or magazines
4 going to the cinema or theatre
5 meeting friends and relatives
6 painting or drawing
7 singing or dancing
8 playing a musical instrument
9 dressmaking, needlework or knitting
10 collecting things (e.g. stamps, books)
11 walking or trekking
12 playing sports or games

Finally, add any other popular activities not listed here.

2 Write a brief justification of your choice of activities.

Structure and Vocabulary Aid

A Referring to a diagram, chart etc.

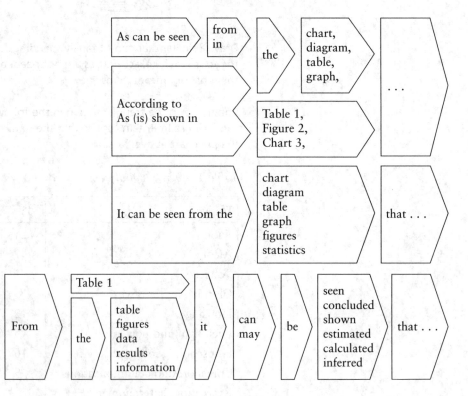

B Describing change

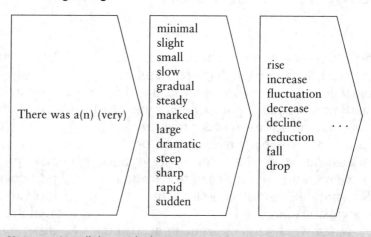

Note: Not all the words above can go with each other e.g. use *steady rise*, **NOT** *steady fluctuation*.

C Comparing

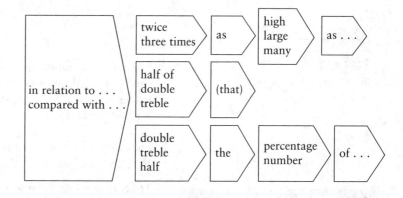

D Useful vocabulary for describing the information in a graph

a *trend* involves a direction
a *curve* involves a shape or position

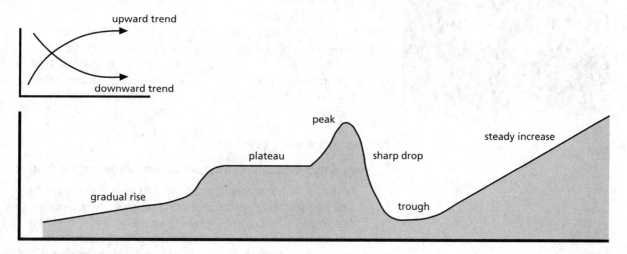

Unit 12　Discussion

So far in these units we have practised parts of the language that are useful for particular purposes. In Units 12 and 13 we shall practise putting together a number of language functions in order to express our ideas. In developing an argument or discussion we need to express our opinion or views, and then we need to conclude. We shall look at introductions and conclusions in Unit 13.

When we discuss or argue in academic writing, we normally need to present a balanced view. We must also ensure that facts and opinions are clearly separated.

We often look at what other people have already said on the same subject or we look at other ideas. Making references to the writing of others is considered in Units 15 and 16.

When reading, we probably look at the advantages and disadvantages of a particular idea or proposal or action; we look at arguments for (or in favour) and against. Then we try to evaluate the different opinions, comparing and contrasting, and eventually give our own opinions (see the Structure and Vocabulary Aid).

Stage 1
'For' and 'Against'

There are several different methods of teaching a subject. They can be divided into two broad categories: teacher-centred and student-centred. Here we shall look at one example of a teacher-centred method.

1 Look at the following notes. Can you think of any other arguments to add to the lists? If so, write them down.

Lecturing as a Method of Teaching

For	**Against**
a Lectures are an economical way of giving information to a large number of students.	a Lectures are often badly delivered and are boring.
b The latest information or views can be heard.	b Often the same lecture notes are used year after year.
c It is more interesting to hear and see a person than to read a book.	c It is difficult to take notes in a lecture.
d A good lecture can stimulate thought and discussion.	d Many lecturers just read aloud parts of their books. It is easier to read the books.

2 Read the following passage carefully.

Advantages and Disadvantages of the Lecturing Method

Lecturing as a method of teaching is so frequently under attack today from educational psychologists and by students that some justification is needed to retain it. Critics believe that it results in passive methods of learning which tend to be
5　less effective than those which fully engage the learner. They

also maintain that students have no opportunity to ask questions and must all receive the same content at the same pace, that they are exposed only to one teacher's interpretation of subject matter which will inevitably be
10 biased and that, anyway, few lectures rise above dullness. Nevertheless, in a number of inquiries this pessimistic assessment of lecturing as a teaching method proves not to be general among students, although they do fairly often comment on poor lecturing techniques.
15   Students praise lectures which are clear, orderly synopses in which basic principles are emphasised, but dislike too numerous digressions or lectures which consist in part of the contents of a textbook. Students of science subjects consider that a lecture is a good way to introduce a new subject,
20 putting it in its context, or to present material not yet included in books. They also appreciate its value as a period of discussion of problems and possible solutions with their lecturer. They do not look for inspiration – this is more commonly mentioned by teachers – but arts students look for
25 originality in lectures. Medical and dental students who have reported on teaching methods, or specifically on lecturing, suggest that there should be fewer lectures or that, at the least, more would be unpopular.

3 The writer of the passage above is evaluating the different views held by different groups of students. The style of writing is impersonal and a number of generalisations are used. Write a paragraph adding your own view of lecturing. You can begin (in the following impersonal way):

One of the main arguments | against | lecturing is that . . .
                                  | in favour of |

Pyramid Discussion
Taking Notes in Lectures

1 Select the three most important reasons for taking notes in lectures from the following list. The order of the choices is not important.

> **Note:** Information about organising a Pyramid Discussion is given in the Guide to Using the Book.

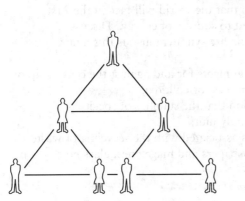

1 to remember exactly what was said
2 to record useful information accurately
3 to help understand ideas
4 to develop the ability to summarise quickly
5 to act as a reminder in the future
6 to keep a record of different points of view
7 to focus attention on certain points
8 to help organise information on topics
9 to provide brief information for revision purposes
10 to give guidance for writing essays
11 to provide an overview of a topic
12 to help your concentration in the lecture

13 to help increase your writing speed
14 to provide a framework for follow-up reading on the subject
15 to support or compare with previous information and ideas

Finally, add some reasons of your own that are not included in the list above.

2 Write a passage describing the main advantages and problems of taking notes in lectures. In the final paragraph give your own views.

Stage 2
Starting with Notes

1 Some notes on advertising follow. Making use of the notes, write about advertising, presenting the arguments for and against. Add your own view at the end. You will probably need to compare and contrast and to make qualified generalisations.

Advertising

For

a Advertisements give up-to-date information about products.
b If there was no advertising consumers would only know about goods in their local shops.
c Advertising helps to sell to a bigger market. Therefore, as more goods are sold they are cheaper.
d Advertisements provide revenue for newspapers etc.

Against

a Advertisements do not give information, they try to persuade us to buy.
b They create a demand for goods that are not really needed.
c Advertising adds to the cost of the goods.
d Advertisements are generally ugly to look at and spoil the environment.

2 Choose one of the following topics to write about. Before you begin, make notes **for** and **against** aspects of the subject. Discuss both sides of the argument, comparing and contrasting. Where necessary, make qualified generalisations. You may wish to mention cause and effect. Try to give reasons for your own view at the end.

– Discuss the function of newspapers.
– 'The biggest problem that the world will face in the 21st century will be related to sources of energy.' Discuss.
– 'Business and pollution are synonymous.' Is this a fair comment? Discuss.
– Evaluate the main arguments for and against the censorship of films and TV programmes for children.
– Discuss the proposition that the stability of society is maintained by the family unit.
– Discuss the problems associated with the recycling of waste material such as newspapers and magazines, glass bottles and drink cans.

- What are the difficulties in trying to compare the standard of living between countries?
- Are exams unfair? Is continuous assessment a fairer way to measure progress? Discuss.

> **Note:** Refer to Glossary of examination and essay questions in Unit 19 if necessary.

3 Choose some aspects of your own specialised subject or a subject in which you are interested and write a discussion.

Stage 3
Ideas from Texts

1 Sometimes we may read an article in a journal or a passage in a book which may stimulate us to think and then compare our opinions with the writer's views. If we examine the areas where we agree and disagree this can lead to an interesting discussion in writing. Read the following passage from *Social Principles and the Democratic State* by Benn and Peters (George Allen & Unwin, London, 1959). Think about the implications, decide your own views, make notes, and then write an answer to the question: Is there such a thing as an international society?

> IS THERE AN INTERNATIONAL SOCIETY?
> The concept of an international society is not, on the face of it, one towards which men are attracted by strong sentiments or lasting traditions. There is no international 'image' to parallel the national 'image'. The solidarity felt by members of a nation–state with persons or groups outside its frontiers is generally far weaker than the sentiment of nationality, and can rarely compete with it effectively. The over-riding solidarity of the international proletariat, which Marx urges in the 'Communist Manifesto', has been shown in two World Wars to be still a wish, not a reality. Nevertheless, there may still be an international order, though of a weaker sort than the national orders.

2 Think of an idea or passage in a book or journal that has stimulated you to think strongly in support of it or against it. Quote the idea or passage, if possible (and give full references), and write in favour of it or against it, giving your reasons.

Structure and Vocabulary Aid

A Marking stages in a discussion

In summarising the stages in a discussion or in presenting your arguments, you can mark the order of the items or degrees of importance by certain words or phrases. Some examples are:

First, Firstly, First of all, In the first place, The most important . . .
Second, Secondly, In the second place, The next most important . . .
Next, Then, After this/that, Following this/that . . .
Finally, Lastly, In conclusion . . .

> **Note:** Points of view may be expressed cautiously or tentatively (see Unit 10), or strongly or emphatically (it depends upon your feelings and the purpose of the writing). Agreement or disagreement may be total or partial. Below are some ways of expressing your views.

B Introducing your own point of view

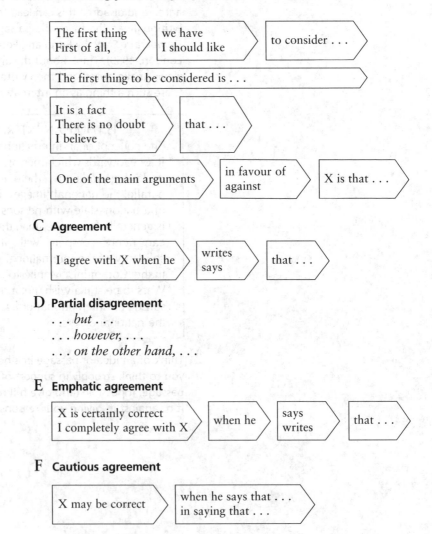

The first thing / First of all, → we have / I should like → to consider . . .

The first thing to be considered is . . .

It is a fact / There is no doubt / I believe → that . . .

One of the main arguments → in favour of / against → X is that . . .

C Agreement

I agree with X when he → writes / says → that . . .

D Partial disagreement

. . . but . . .
. . . however, . . .
. . . on the other hand, . . .

E Emphatic agreement

X is certainly correct / I completely agree with X → when he → says / writes → that . . .

F Cautious agreement

X may be correct → when he says that . . . / in saying that . . .

G Disagreement

> I disagree with X when he says that . . .

H Emphasis by grammatical inversion

One way of giving emphasis to what is written is by using a grammatical construction sometimes known as 'negative inversion'. Some of the introductory words are listed below. If they are used, the word order after the introductory words should be inverted as in the example:

Rarely had such a noise been heard.
Never . . .
Hardly . . . when . . .
Not only . . . but also . . .
Under no circumstances . . .
On no account . . .
Seldom . . .
Neither . . .
Few . . .
Little . . .

Unit 13 Introductions and Conclusions

The introduction, especially the introductory paragraph, is important for a number of reasons. If it is clearly constructed, it will create a good impression on the reader. A good introduction will not be too long, but its length will vary according to the type of writing. In an essay it may be a maximum of half a page (divided into paragraphs); in a dissertation it may be several pages. It will indicate the structure of the writing by giving an overview of the content in sequence. It may introduce the subject, perhaps with a definition or some historical background.

A conclusion is needed to show that the writing is finished. Drawing a conclusion often involves making a summary of the main points already made. This may include commenting on the implications arising from the main body of the writing: possibly indicating that further research is needed in certain areas or that certain action is needed. In addition, one's own opinion or viewpoint may be added, if it is appropriate to do so.

A common mistake is to add a conclusion that does not follow logically from what has been written before. (This is sometimes called a 'non-sequitur'.) Avoid doing this! Also avoid introducing a new argument into the conclusion and do not give (more) examples. Before writing any of the exercises look at the Structure and Vocabulary Aid at the end of this unit. The Notes on the Exercises contain comments on some of the exercises.

Stage 1
Introductory Paragraphs

1 Read the following introductory paragraph to an essay and then discuss it with other students. Why is it a poor beginning?

Essay title: **Discuss the problems of pollution in your country.**

Since the current trend of 'Green' politics came to the fore, we have discovered our water is unfit for consumption; our meat is poisoned by various bacteria; and our fruit and vegetables are contaminated by chemicals. Not only are food and water affected, but the land and sea are constantly subject to chemical and nuclear dumping. In addition, sewage and various oil disasters have contributed to the increase in the killing of wildlife. Even the air we breathe is polluted every day by the millions of cars constantly pumping carbon monoxide into the atmosphere.

2   The following introductory paragraph is on the same subject. Read
    it and then discuss it. Why is it better than the one above?

Despite the increased awareness of the problems of
pollution in recent years, Britain continues to trail
behind most of Western Europe in adopting stricter
measures of control. While it is almost impossible to
consider the problems of pollution with respect to one
country in isolation, the most serious problems to
affect Britain directly are probably those of industrial
and nuclear waste, pesticides and car exhaust fumes.
In what follows, each of these will be discussed
together with their effects. Finally, it will be argued
that to continue to ignore such problems is at the
peril not only of Britain's environment but of the
environment in general.

3   As a result of reading the two paragraphs and your discussions, try
    to write a better-structured paragraph on the same topic for your
    country.

4   Below are two introductory paragraphs that might begin the essay
    on the title given. Both of the paragraphs have been written by
    native English-speakers. Read the paragraphs carefully and decide
    which one you think is best, and why. Discuss your views with other
    students to see if you agree.

Essay title: **Discuss the present-day problems facing secondary
education in your country.**

a   There are, of course, two sectors of secondary
    education in England and Wales: the private sector
    and the state sector. This essay will be concerned
    only with the latter since it is by far the larger and
    is faced with many more problems. These can be
    traced to two important sources: a rapidly changing
    society and a lack of resources.

b   This essay will examine the problems facing secondary
    education in Britain today. It will examine the background
    to the problems, starting with the 1944 Education Act,
    which established universal free primary and secondary
    education. It will then look at problems associated with
    comprehensive schools. After this, it will examine the
    concept of the National Curriculum, the extended
    responsibilities and powers of school governors and the
    local management of schools. Finally, there will be an
    analysis of the relationship between central government and
    local education authorities, and a discussion of the problems
    relating to the financing of schools.

5 Now write an introductory paragraph for the same essay title about your country.

Stage 2
Concluding Remarks

Look at this structure for an essay on the topic 'Examinations hinder education. Discuss.' Read through the notes, decide your own views on the subject and then write a concluding paragraph.

Note: *hinder* means delay, slow down, prevent

Essay title: **Examinations hinder education. Discuss.**

Notes

Introduction:
- Some assessment of teaching/learning needed.
- What is the best kind/method?

Advantages of exams:
- A well-established system.
- Reliable and usually quick.
- Marked anonymously, therefore no favouritism.
- Constantly being improved.
- Not subjective, therefore fair.
- Often objective tests are used.
- They provide a clear aim or purpose.
- An easy and cheap method of evaluation.

Disadvantages of exams:
- A primitive method of testing knowledge and ability.
- Should test what you know, often they do the opposite.
- A test of memory, not ability or aptitude.
- Not enough time.
- They cause anxiety and unnecessary stress.
- Students are judged by exam results not education received.
- They restrict teachers' freedom; waste time teaching exam techniques.
- They cause unnecessary and wasteful competition.

Possible conclusion: ?

Stage 3
Concluding from Tables

1 Look carefully at the information in Tables 1 and 2 below. Are there any general conclusions that you can draw comparing males and females, and the periods 1950–1955 with 1990–1995?

2 Select any two countries you wish for the purpose of making a comparison. Briefly state the comparison you are making and then draw appropriate conclusions from the data.

Table 1: Infant mortality rates* (Source: Philip's Geographical Digest 1996-97, Heinemann Educational, 1996)

Country	1950–1955	1990–1995
Australia	24	7
Denmark	28	6
India	190	88
Japan	51	5
Kenya	150	64
Mexico	114	36
New Zealand	26	9
Poland	95	17
Saudi Arabia	200	58
Sierra Leone	231	143
Thailand	132	24
UK	28	8
USA	28	8

* Infant mortality rate = deaths of infants under one year old per 1000 live births.

Table 2: Life expectancy (age) (Source: Philip's Geographical Digest 1996–97, Heinemann Educational, 1996)

Country	Sex	1950–1955	1990–1995
Australia	male	67	74
	female	72	80
Denmark	male	70	73
	female	72	79
India	male	39	60
	female	38	61
Japan	male	62	76
	female	66	82
Kenya	male	39	59
	female	43	63
Mexico	male	49	67
	female	52	74
New Zealand	male	68	73
	female	72	79
Poland	male	59	68
	female	64	76
Saudi Arabia	male	39	64
	female	41	68
Sierra Leone	male	29	41
	female	32	45
Thailand	male	45	65
	female	49	69
UK	male	67	73
	female	72	79
USA	male	66	73
	female	72	80

3 Study the following table, which gives information about children killed in road accidents in Britain during May, June and July in one recent year. Comment on the significant items and discuss them. What conclusions can you draw?

Table 3: Road accidents in Britain

When/Where accidents occurred	Age 2–4	Age 5–7	Age 8–11	Age 11–13	Age 14–16	TOTAL
Going to school	2	12	8	2	1	25
Going home from school	2	17	10	3	2	34
Playing in the street	98	81	28	5	2	214
Cycling in the street	1	10	25	8	1	45
Shopping for their parents	5	32	12	2	1	52
TOTAL	108	152	83	20	7	370

Structure and Vocabulary Aid

A Introductions

A variety of ways are possible. Introductions commonly include these elements:

> stating the topic
> description of   – problem to be considered
>   – historical background
>   – structure of the writing and sequence of the main points
> definition and/or explanation of the subject

For example: *In this essay X will be examined. First the arguments in favour will be considered and then the arguments against. Finally, it will be shown that Y appears to be the biggest problem.*

B Summarising and concluding

In short, . . .	In conclusion, . . .
In a word, . . .	On the whole, . . .
In brief, . . .	Altogether, . . .
To sum up, . . .	In all, . . .

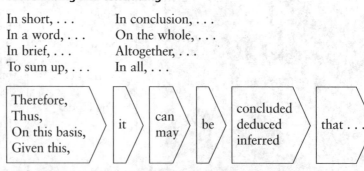

Therefore, / Thus, / On this basis, / Given this, > it > can / may > be > concluded / deduced / inferred > that . . .

Note: See also examples of 'cautious' language used in the Structure and Vocabulary Aid of Unit 10, e.g.

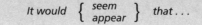

It would { *seem / appear* } *that . . .*

C Useful vocabulary

1 Stating the topic

concept	hypothesise	proposition
to consist	issue	to speculate
factor	to predict	thesis
hypothesis	premise	topic

2 General research vocabulary

academic	evidence	reliable
anecdotal	exception	research
anomaly	explicit	source
argument	feasible	study
assimilate	findings	subsequent
cogent	homogeneous	survey
conform	implicit	tentative
consequent	issue	theory
controversy	norm	trend
debate	pertinent	valid
empirical	principle	
to equate	relevance	

3 Reporting verbs

to add	to deny	to postulate
to affirm	to describe	to query
to agree	to determine	to question
to argue	to disagree	to recommend
to assert	to discern	to refute
to assume	to discuss	to reject
to challenge	to dispute	to remark
to claim	to emphasise	to report
to clarify	to enumerate	to repudiate
to comment	to explain	to say
to consider	to imply	to suggest
to contend	to infer	to stipulate
to contradict	to maintain	to view
to demonstrate	to point out	

(Based on 'Concordancing and the Teaching of the Vocabulary of Academic English' by J. Thurstun and C.N. Candlin in *English for Specific Purposes*, Vol. 17, No. 3, 1998)

Unit 14   Academic Style

Written English, like spoken English, may be formal or informal. The main features of academic writing are as follows: it is formal in an impersonal or objective style (often using impersonal pronouns and phrases and passive verb forms); cautious language is frequently used in reporting research and making claims; vocabulary appropriate for particular academic contexts is used (this may involve specialist or technical words); the structure of the writing will vary according to the particular type (genre), for example, essay, report, thesis, etc. In addition, academic writing often contains references to other writers' publications, sometimes including quotations (this will be looked at in Units 15 and 16).

It is important to remember that writing styles (formal and informal) should not be mixed: there should be uniformity and consistency. Besides this, the language should be appropriate for the context. (See the Structure and Vocabulary Aid at the end of this unit for more details.)

Stage 1
Informal and Formal

1   Compare these two explanations or definitions of economics. What are the main differences?

Informal/Spoken. Economics? Yes, well, . . . economics is, I suppose, about people trying to . . . let me see . . . match things that are scarce, you know, with things that they want, . . . oh, yes, and how these efforts have an effect on each other . . . through exchange, I suppose.

Formal/Written. Economics is the social science that studies how people attempt to accommodate scarcity to their wants and how these attempts interact through exchange.

2   The following sentences are mixed formal and informal. Write F (formal) or I (informal) in the brackets after each sentence.

a   The project will be completed next year. ( )
b   I showed that his arguments did not hold water. ( )
c   I wonder why he put up with those terrible conditions for so long. ( )
d   Five more tests will be necessary before the experiment can be concluded. ( )
e   It is possible to consider the results from a different viewpoint. ( )
f   It has been proved that the arguments so far are without foundation. ( )
g   He'll have to do another five tests before he can stop the experiment. ( )
h   It isn't clear why such terrible conditions were tolerated for so long. ( )
i   There are a number of reasons why the questionnaire should be revised. ( )
j   We'll finish the job next year. ( )

3 The following sentences are all informal. Rewrite them in a formal style. (See the Structure and Vocabulary Aid at the end of this unit.)

   a She said it wasn't good enough.
   b I thought the lecture was terribly difficult to follow.
   c They've got to find out how to carry out a survey of old folks' opinions of little kids.
   d The results were a lot better than I expected.
   e None of our other student friends knew the answer either.
   f He said: 'It's hell being on your own.'

4 **Cautious language** is important in academic writing. Look at the following sentences, which all contain definite statements. Rewrite the sentences so that the statements are more cautious. This will involve changing the verb forms and/or adding appropriate qualifying adverbs, adjectives or nouns (see the Structure and Vocabulary Aid for Unit 10).

   a A survey has shown that lecturers use the terms 'seminars' and 'tutorials' interchangeably.
   b The rate of inflation will not increase this year.
   c Reading is effective when it has a particular purpose.
   d The answer to problems is found in asking the right questions.
   e Countries disagree on the interpretation of democracy.

Stage 2
Different Styles

1 Look at these eight explanations or definitions of 'education', written in different styles.

  – Decide if the explanations are spoken or written.
  – Match each one with the source from which you think it is taken, listed at the end.

What is education?

   a Education can be seen either as a battlefield for values or a question of systems or, more simply, as an extension of the biological function of the upbringing of children – known more simply as parenting. We'll start by looking at how far the role of teacher goes beyond being a parent.
   b The process by which your mind develops through learning at a school, college, or university; the knowledge and skills that you gain from being taught.
   c 'Education' comes from a Latin word. One of the important things about education is to give people an interest in knowledge and an ability to learn – or strategies or techniques for learning – and a knowledge of how to find out about things they want to know.
   d Education: teaching, schooling, training, instruction, tuition, tutelage, edification, tutoring, cultivation, upbringing, indoctrination, drilling; learning, lore, knowledge, information, erudition . . .
   e 'Tis Education forms the common mind,
      Just as the twig is bent, the tree's inclin'd.

f   Central to the concept of education is the development of knowledge and understanding. In schools and universities explicit attempts are made to do this by means of an organised sequence of learning experiences which is called the curriculum. But what should be its priorities? Should the depth of knowledge or breadth be the ideal? . . .

g   People going to school and learning.

h   Education . . . has produced a vast population able to read but unable to distinguish what is worth reading.

Sources:

1   Spoken – a simple explanation by an adult.
2   *The Oxford Thesaurus* (An A–Z Dictionary of Synonyms), Oxford University Press, 1991
3   *Longman Dictionary of Contemporary English*, 1995
4   *English Social History*, G.M. Trevelyan, Longmans Green & Co., 1962
5   Spoken – a considered explanation by an educated adult.
6   Spoken – an introduction to a lecture on education.
7   *The Philosophy of Education* – Introduction by Prof. R.S. Peters, Oxford University Press, 1973
8   From a poem in 1734 by Alexander Pope (1688–1744).

2   Now write your own explanation of 'education' in an academic style.

3   Look at these eight explanations or definitions of 'poverty'. Discuss with another student the distinguishing features of the different explanations (spoken or written) and try to identify the type of source for each. Give reasons for your decisions.

What is Poverty?

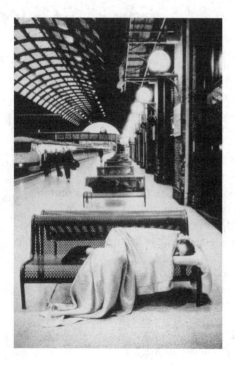

a   The situation or experience of being poor.

b   It is the inability to attain a minimal standard of living. It can be expressed either in absolute terms (total numbers living below a certain per capita income level) or relative terms (compared with the average standard of living of the country as a whole). First we will consider absolute poverty.

c   When poverty comes in at the door, love flies out of the window.

d   The situation facing those in society whose material needs are least satisfied. Poverty can be defined by some absolute measure . . . or in relative terms . . . In either case it is necessarily an arbitrarily defined concept.

e   It means not having enough to live on in terms of food and shelter and the other basic necessities of life.

f   The poor old man is badly off; he's always hard up and needs everything he can get.

g   The greatest of evils and the worst of crimes is poverty.

h   The Social Surveys of London, Liverpool and other towns round about 1929 showed that there remained perhaps ten per cent of the urban population below the 'poverty line', even outside the depressed areas.

4 Now write your own explanation of 'poverty' in an academic style.

5 In an academic style write an explanation or definition of one of these:

democracy	money	language
boredom	crime	development
happiness	death	

Stage 3
Inappropriate Language

The following passage is written in a mixed style with some colloquialisms and other inappropriate words. Rewrite it in an academic style with appropriate vocabulary, structures and cautious language.

Causes of Writing Errors

Research has shown (James) that learners of English find writing the most difficult thing they've got to do. There are 3 main types of error that the learner will make.

The biggest sort of error leads to misunderstanding or a total
5 breakdown in communication. There are lots of causes of this: the biggest is the use of translation from the mother tongue. By translating word for word the student uses the wrong sentence patterns (grammar) and the wrong words (vocabulary). Another cause is choosing to write long and complicated sentences
10 with far too many supplementary clauses. The longer the sentence the bigger is the chance of making mistakes and failing to communicate the meaning. Therefore, in the early stages of your writing, you shouldn't write sentences longer than 3 lines.

Structure and
Vocabulary Aid

A Informal style

In general, informal English contains a number of colloquialisms (conversational expressions) that are inappropriate for formal written English. It is important not to mix styles.

Written academic English will **not** normally contain the following:
– Contractions (i.e. *it did not* would be used instead of *it didn't*; *they have* would be used and not *they've*).
– Hesitation fillers (e.g. *well, you know . . .*) which might be common in the spoken language are omitted.
– A number of phrasal or prepositional verbs are more suitable for an informal style and are therefore inappropriate in academic writing, e.g.

formal	informal
conduct	carry out
discover	find out
investigate	look into

– Euphemisms (words which are thought to be less unpleasant and less direct) are often used informally but should be avoided in academic writing. For example:

direct	euphemism
to die	to pass away
to tell lies/to lie	to tell falsehoods/fibs
ill	poorly
old person	senior citizen

Personal pronouns *I*, *you*, *we* tend not to be used in more formal writing (except in letters, etc.). Instead the style may be more impersonal. An introductory *it* or *there* may begin sentences or even the impersonal pronoun *one*; passive verb tenses may also be used.

B Academic style

Academic English frequently uses language that is cautious or tentative. The language forms commonly used are listed in the Structure and Vocabulary Aid for Unit 10. The main forms covered are:

– Modal verbs (e.g *may*, *might*, *will*, *would*, *can*, *could*)
– Lexical verbs (e.g. *seem*, *appear*, *suggest*, *indicate*, *assume*, *believe*)
– Modal adverbs (e.g. *perhaps*, *probably*, *possibly*, *apparently*)
– Modal adjectives (e.g. *probable*, *possible*, *(un)certain*)
– Modal nouns (e.g. *assumption*, *claim*, *evidence*, *estimate*, *possibility*)

Unit 15   Paraphrasing and Summarising

In many types of academic writing it is often necessary to refer to other people's research. This may be done to give support to your own research or ideas. Direct quotations from books and articles are considered in Unit 16. In this unit we shall look at and practise paraphrasing (using your own words to report someone else's writing, but maintaining an academic style) and summarising (giving a brief account of the main points of some writing). In both of these it will be necessary to look for topic sentences and keywords in the original texts (the main information/points).

References must always be given to the sources of the texts you are making use of (see Unit 16), otherwise you may be accused of plagiarism (using someone else's ideas or words as if they were your own). Advice on making summaries is contained in the Structure and Vocabulary Aid at the end of this unit.

Stage 1
Paraphrase

Rewriting a text for the purpose of including it in your own writing can be done in several ways. Look at these examples and then do the exercises.

1   By changing the vocabulary (verbs/nouns)

    e.g.   She examined the difficulties that . . .

        = *She investigated the problems that . . .*

Rewrite the following:

Smith and Jones (1991) found that the circumstances had . . .

2   By changing the verb form (e.g. from active to passive: this can change the focus or emphasis)

    e.g.   Johns (1987) analysed the students' difficulties and . . .

        = *The students' difficulties were analysed by Johns (1987) and . . .*

> **Note:**   Using a passive rather than an active verb form here changes the focus from the writer to the research i.e. the students' difficulties.

Rewrite the following:

Brown and White (1994) observed the problems caused by seminars . . .

3   By changing the word class (e.g. from verb to noun phrase)

    e.g.   The reports were completed in April . . .

        = *The completion of the reports in April ensured that the students had time to revise before their examination.*

Suggest a different continuation after:

The completion of the reports in April . . .

> **Note:**   Changing the word class allows you to add your own comments.

Rewrite the following and add an appropriate comment of your own:

James and Harris (1984) concluded that there was a need for note-taking practice.

4 By synthesis

You may need to combine two or more viewpoints or pieces of information from other writers in your paraphrase and summary. Often one reference will support another, but there may be opposing views as well.

Example of a synthesis

Johns and Dudley-Evans (1980) touched on the problems created by the lecturers' use of colloquial words and phrases . . . This use of informal language was also noted by Jackson and Bilton (1994) who investigated geology lectures given in English . . .

Two direct quotations are given below relating to the same topic (note taking). Paraphrase and combine them in a brief report (not using direct quotations). See the Structure and Vocabulary Aid for a selection of reporting verbs.

'Terseness of note taking . . . rather than mere quantity seems to be an essential ingredient of effective . . . note taking. (Dunkel, 1988)

'several other researchers have found similar positive relationships between "terseness" of notes and test performance . . .' (Chaudron, Loschky and Cook, 1994)

| Note: | *terseness* here means being brief or concise. |

Stage 2
Summary

1 Read this passage. Which is the topic/main sentence?

Culture Shock

'Culture shock' is the state of being confused when in contact with a different and unfamiliar civilization. 'Shock' suggests something that is negative: this may be true, especially at first. Typically, a person going to study in another country for the first time may miss family and friends and, consequently, feel homesick. The person may have sleeping difficulties and, in extreme cases, may become depressed or ill.

2 Now read this summary of the passage above. Discuss why it is a reasonable summary. Is there anything you would change?

Culture shock is the confusion caused by contact with an alien society. Initially, reactions may be negative.

3 Summarise the main aspects of culture shock that you or your friends have experienced.

4 Read the following passage on Leisure Activities. Make notes on it and summarise it: rewrite it as one sentence (maximum length one-third of the original).

Leisure Activities

In Britain, the most common leisure activities take place at home and include entertaining friends and relatives. Watching television is by far the most popular pastime as 99% of homes have a TV set, and the average viewing time is about 26 hours a week. In addition, using and hiring video tapes is also very popular, with 80% of homes having a video recorder. Listening to the radio is virtually universal as almost every home has a radio; it is listened to, on average, about 16 hours a week.

5 Now very briefly describe the most popular leisure activities in your country.

Stage 3
Different Viewpoints

1 Read the passage below on Rural Tourism, make notes on it and then summarise the advantages and disadvantages in two sentences.

Rural Tourism: For and Against

Johnson (1971) has listed two major advantages of tourism in rural areas. The first is economic: tourism creates employment. The jobs are mainly in the travel industry, hotels, guest houses, restaurants and cafes. However, visitors spend their money in
5 a variety of ways which affect other jobs indirectly. For example, by buying local souvenirs and gifts, tourists help to support local shops. The second advantage of tourism is the support that the income provides for local services and amenities. Because large numbers of visitors use the local
10 buses etc. it makes it possible to keep these buses running for local people.

As well as advantages there are also three main disadvantages of tourism (Walker, 1982). The first is erosion of the countryside by so many people: paths, grass and other
15 areas of vegetation and woodland get worn away. In addition, tourist traffic causes congestion and obstruction and delays local people doing their work. Finally, an influx of tourists causes pollution problems in many areas. The pollution can take many forms but the main ones are the exhaust fumes of
20 vehicles which pollute the atmosphere, and the litter that people leave behind, such as tin cans, plastic and paper, and bottles.

2 Describe briefly how tourism has affected a particular place in your country.

Pyramid Discussion
Tourism and International Understanding

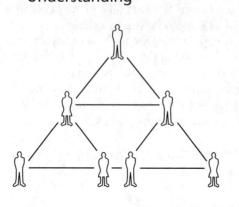

1 Which are the three main ways in which tourism helps to develop understanding between countries? Select from the list below. The order of the choices is not important.

1 contact between people helps understanding
2 increases cultural awareness
3 experience of different food, drink, etc.
4 develops a sense of historical awareness
5 cheaper travel enables more people to meet
6 national stereotypes or prejudices are broken down
7 different economic and social systems are more easily understood
8 interest in different ways of life is stimulated
9 the sale of more goods benefits countries
10 people are influenced by what they see

Finally, add any other ways you can think of to the list above.

2 How important do you think tourism is for international understanding? Write a brief discussion of the main points.

Structure and Vocabulary Aid

A Reporting verbs

Look at these examples of reporting verbs commonly used in paraphrases and summaries. The verb tense can vary in many cases to suit the nature of what you are writing.

As X	observes	...
	has observed	
	observed	
	had observed	
	points out	
	remarks	
	says	
	states	
	affirms	
X	argues	that ...
	assumes	
	believes	
	claims	
	concludes	
	explains	
	finds	
	implies	
	maintains	
	suggests	

Other structures:

As noted by X . . .
According to X . . .
It has been argued by X that . . .
In X's view . . .

> **Note:** Other reporting verbs are included in the Structure and Vocabulary Aid in Unit 13. These reporting verbs and structures can be used to introduce quotations as well (see Unit 16).

B Advice and suggestions for writing summaries

- At the beginning write the title of the book/journal, the author and article, publisher and date.
- Quickly read (skim) the text to get an overall idea of it.
- Then read it carefully, identifying the main points.
- As you read, make brief notes of the main points – note the keywords and topic sentences (i.e. the main ones) – in your own words as far as possible, using synonyms where appropriate (i.e. paraphrase).
- If certain sentences or phrases are important and may be useful to quote in an essay etc., copy them exactly, word for word, and put them in inverted commas (quotation marks). If you intend to abbreviate the quotation by omitting some words, put three dots (. . .) in place of the words.
- Remove examples and details, including dates (unless vitally important, e.g. an invention, a change of process/procedure).
- Ensure that your summary is accurate and neutral, i.e. do not add your own views to it (these can follow later).
- As far as possible condense the points into straightforward statements and rewrite in your own words where possible.
- Write clearly, concisely, coherently and logically.

> **Note:** A thesaurus or a dictionary of synonyms can be useful at times when paraphrasing.

Unit 16   Quotations and Referencing

Direct quotations and references to authors' writings are often included in essays, reports, dissertations and theses. They are included to show that you have read around the subject and are aware of what has been written about it. Their purpose is also to demonstrate support for your own ideas, points of view and findings, and perhaps to show examples or evidence.

  Quotations should not be overused: your own writing is more important to your teacher or supervisor. However, when you do include quotations they should be acknowledged with the correct reference conventions and listed at the end of your writing. These conventions may vary a little from place to place (they need to be checked) but the main ones are practised and shown in this unit. It is important to acknowledge the source of the quotations otherwise you may be accused of plagiarism. The conventions of paraphrasing were looked at in Unit 15. The reference system is the same as shown here.

  Before beginning the exercises below, look at the information on quotations and references in the Structure and Vocabulary Aid at the end of this unit.

Stage 1
Bibliography

1   It is important that references are arranged in strict **alphabetical order**. It is usually necessary to include the first names or initial letters of authors in addition to their surnames. Surnames beginning with *Mc* are treated as if their spelling was *Mac* e.g. McKenzie, like Mackenzie, will come before Madison.

The following surnames (and initials) are those of authors of books. Number the names in each list in alphabetical order from 1 to 12.

LIST A		LIST B	
Dawson, E.	____	Johns, T.F.	____
Davidson, D.	____	James, K.	____
Davey, A.C.	____	Johnson, R.	____
Davies, C.T.	____	Jones, J.F.	____
Day, D.A.	____	Johnston, S.A.	____
Davey, A.M.	____	Jackson, J.	____
Dawkins, R.	____	Johnson, K.	____
Davis, A.	____	James, C.V.	____
Davidson, G.D.	____	Johns, A.M.	____
Davies, C.W.	____	Jones, C.	____
Davy, A.	____	Johns, C.	____
Dawes, C.G.	____	James, D.V.	____

2 There are a number of errors in the bibliography or list of references below. These may be to do with the order of items or the omission of some details. Mark the places where the errors occur and then write a description of the error and what is needed to correct it.

> Abbott, G. (1981). Encouraging communication in English: a paradox. *ELT Journal.*
>
> James, K. (1984a). The writing of theses by speakers of English as a Foreign Language: the results of a case study. In R. Williams, J. Swales and J. Kirkman (Eds.). *Common ground: shared interests in ESP and communication studies. ELT documents: 117.*
>
> James (1984b). *Speak to Learn.*
>
> McDonough, J. (1984). *ESP in Perspective: A Practical Guide.* Collins ELT: London.
>
> Mackay, R. & A. Mountford (Eds.) (1978). *English for Specific Purposes.* London: Longman.
>
> Zamel, V. Responding to student writing. *TESOL Quarterly*, 19 (1).
>
> Swales, J.M. (1995). The role of the textbook in EAP writing research. *English for Specific Purposes*, 14 (1).
>
> Swales, J.M. and C.B. Feak (1994). *Academic Writing for Graduate Students.* Ann Arbor: University of Michigan Press.

3 Write a short bibliography for your subject, listing five to ten books and articles. Ensure that all the details are correct.

Stage 2
Quotations and References

1 Read the following passage carefully. Notice the different ways in which the quotations are used and how they are acknowledged. Notice also how the references are listed at the end.

- From how many different sources are direct quotations made?
- From how many different sources are paraphrases made?

Writer's Block and Getting Started

A writer's block is the feeling of being unable to write. It is different from writer's cramp, which is stiffness of the hand caused by writing for a long time. Three different kinds of block have been diagnosed: physical, procedural and
5 psychological (Smith, 1982). Beard and Hartley (1984:258) have neatly summarised the main differences:

> Physical blocks occur when the writer is tired and it just becomes too much of an effort to continue. Procedural blocks occur when the writer cannot decide what to write
> 10 next. Psychological blocks occur when the words should come, and could come, but the writer cannot bring himself or herself to let the words appear on the paper.

One of the main difficulties in writing for native speakers of English is the process of 'getting started'. A questionnaire was
15 sent to academics at a university in England and one in Canada by Hartley and Knapper (1984:158). They posed the question 'What do you like least about writing?' A common response was : 'Writing the first paragraph'. Hartley and Knapper commented that 'Almost every respondent confessed
20 to experiencing writer's blocks'.

If writing the first paragraph presents difficulties for native speakers of English, the problem for non-native speakers of English must be at least as great. This was confirmed by Jordan (1993:75) who conducted a survey by questionnaire of
25 overseas students studying at a British university. Based on their experience in their own countries when writing an essay, 67% of the students admitted to having difficulty in starting.

Various suggestions have been made to overcome the
30 problem of 'getting started' in writing. One fairly common one is to begin by simply jotting down ideas or notes on paper (Hartley and Knapper, 1984; Northedge, 1990). In other words, to get what you want to say down on paper as quickly as possible. 'Editing, polishing, changing, resequencing and
35 the like can be left until later. At this stage it does not matter if sentences are incomplete.' (Beard and Hartley, 1984:253)

References

Beard, R.M. and J. Hartley (1984: 4th ed.). *Teaching and Learning in Higher Education.* London: Harper and Row.
40 Hartley, J. and C.K. Knapper (1984). Academics and their Writing. *Studies in Higher Education,* 9(2).
Jordan, R.R. (1993). Study Skills: Experience and Expectations. In G.M. Blue (Ed.) *Language, Learning and Success: Studying through English. Developments in ELT.* London: Macmillan,
45 Modern English Teacher and the British Council.
Northedge, A. (1990). *The Good Study Guide.* Milton Keynes: The Open University.
Smith, F. (1982). *Writing and the Writer.* London: Heinemann Educational.

2 Below are various references, quotations, notes and pieces of information on the topic 'Plagiarism and its history'. Write an account of this, making appropriate use of what is provided. Acknowledge the use of sources and list the references correctly at the end, as in the example above.

Plagiarism and its History

To plagiarize = to take words, ideas etc. from someone else's work and use them in your work, as if they were your own ideas.
(Taken from the 3rd edition of *Longman Dictionary of Contemporary English*, 1995, published by Longman Group Limited, Harlow, Essex.)

Tom McArthur (editor) noted in *The Oxford Companion to the English Language* in 1992, published in Oxford by Oxford University Press: The origin of plagiarism – from the obsolete noun 'plagiary' = a 'kidnapper or a kidnapping, theft or a thief of ideas' – from the Latin 'plagiarius' = a kidnapper or literary thief.

First recorded use of 'plagiary' = late sixteenth century. 'Plagiary' and 'plagiarism' appear in the eighteenth century dictionaries of Nathaniel Bailey and Samuel Johnson.

Plagiarism may be unintentional – unawareness of English-speaking academic conventions – acknowledge all sources . . . many study guides etc. give advice, examples, and ways sources cited.

e.g.   Waters, M. and A. Waters – *Study Tasks in English* – 1995 – Cambridge University Press

L. Hamp-Lyons and K.B. Courter – *Research Matters* – Cambridge, Massachusetts – Newbury House in 1984

I. Leki, 1989 – *Academic Writing* – St. Martin's Press, New York

Article by T. Lynch and I. McGrath (Teaching bibliographic documentation skills in *English for Specific Purposes*, Vol.13 No.3, 1993) – clearly sets out format re bibliography – shows different layout for books, journals and other papers.

Structure and Vocabulary Aid

A Quotations

When referring to a book or article, the normal procedure is to give the author's surname, the year of publication in brackets, and the page numbers if necessary. The full reference is then given at the end of the text.

There are two basic ways of using quotations.

1 Quotation marks (inverted commas) are put around the author's actual words, which are then incorporated in the text: this is often used for short quotations, e.g.

Academic writers need to be cautious in their claims. In this respect, vague language is important as 'it allows claims to be made with due caution, modesty, and humility' (Hyland, 1994 : 241)

2 The quotation is indented (it starts further from the margin than the other lines, and it may be in a different type size or style; the quotation marks are usually omitted): this is normally used for longer quotations (three or more lines), e.g.

Jordan (1977 : 240) also draws attention to the necessity for being careful:

> A feature of academic writing is the need to be cautious in one's claims and statements. In other words, you may indicate your certainty and commitment in varying degrees.

This may be done in various ways . . .

> **Note:** Quotations are the exact words of the author, which must be accurate, with the same punctuation and spelling.

B Incorporating quotations in writing

1 The main uses of quotations in writing are as follows:
   - Support for an argument or point of view. *As X has observed '. . .'*
   - Exemplification of the point being made. *Thus, for example, '. . .'*
   - Introduction of a point or viewpoint etc. *According to X, '. . .'*
   - Conclusion of a discussion, analysis, etc. *Therefore X concludes: '. . .'*
   - Explanation of a point, item, etc. *X explains it as follows: '. . .'*

2 There are many verbs and phrases that can be used to introduce quotations in writing. The verbs and structures noted in Unit 15 can be used. Some of the main structures are as follows:
   - *As X observed/pointed out/suggested/noted/indicated '. . .'*
   - *According to X, '. . .'*
   - *For example, X argued that '. . .'*
   - *X suggests that '. . .'*
   - *The need for it is widely recognised: '. . .'*
   - *Writing in 1979, X commented that '. . .'*
   - *To quote X: '. . .'*
   - *Recent research by X shows that '. . .'*

C References and bibliographies

References, at the end of an essay, for example, are arranged in alphabetical order (A–Z) of the author's surname or the name of the organisation. If more than one author has the same surname, they should appear in alphabetical order of the initial of the first name. If more than one reference is given by the same author, then the earlier dated reference will appear first. If two or more references by the same author appear in the same year, they will be labelled in sequence with letters (a, b, c, etc.) after the year. References to one author are normally listed before those of joint authorship of the same author.

There are differences between references to books and references to journals.

- Note the sequence of information commonly used in references to **books**: Author's surname, initials, date (in brackets), title (underlined or in italics), place of publication, publisher. E.g.

Wallace, M.J. (1980). *Study Skills in English*. Cambridge: Cambridge University Press

- Note the sequence of information commonly used in references to articles in **journals**: Author's surname, initials, date (in brackets), title of article, name of journal (underlined or in italics), volume number, issue number, sometimes season or month, sometimes page numbers. E.g.

West, R. (1994). Needs analysis in language teaching. *Language Teaching*, 27 (1): 1–19

> **Note:** Volume and issue numbers may also be written: Vol. 27 no.1

D Footnotes

A footnote is a note at the bottom (or foot) of a page in a book or journal: it is used to explain a word or other item, or to add some special information or a reference. Sometimes footnotes appear at the end of the essay or article, or even at the back of a book.

A small number is written above the word or item in the text. The explanation of the item is then given the same number. If there are two or more footnotes, then they are numbered in sequence 1, 2, 3, etc. If they appear at the foot of each page, the numbering starts again on each page. If they appear at the end of an essay, the numbering is continuous throughout the essay. There are several systems of giving footnotes but this is the simplest:

> . . . has given rise to a school of thought called neo[1]-Marxism
>
> ---
> [1] neo – a new or modern form or development of

> **Note:** It is generally better to avoid using footnotes in your writing if possible, but you need to understand their use.

E Latin words and abbreviations

Latin words and abbreviations are often used in citation terms or in texts.

Latin	short for . . .	English equivalent
c./ca.	circa	about, approximately (e.g. c. 1000)
cf.	confer	compare with
e.g.	exempli gratia	for example, for instance
et al	et alii	and others
etc.	et cetera	and the rest, and all others, and so on
et seq.	et sequens	and the following pages
ibid.*	ibidem	in the same place (used to refer again to a text just referred to)
i.e.	id est	which is to say, in other words, that is
loc. cit.*	loco citato	in the places already mentioned (+ author's name)
N.B.	nota bene	take special note of; note well
op. cit.*	opere citato	in the work already mentioned (+ author's name and page reference)
passim		frequently, in every part, in many places
q.v.*	quod vide	which may be referred to, refer to, see (often used for cross-references in another part of the text)
viz.	videlicet	namely, that is to say, in other words

> **Note:** It is important to understand these abbreviations, as you will see them used in many academic texts. It is not necessary, however, for you to use many of them in your own writing, especially those marked *.

F Common English abbreviations

Ed./Eds.	Editor(s); edited by; edition
ff.	and the following pages, lines, etc.
l./ll.	line(s)
ms./mss.	manuscript(s)
no./nos.	number(s)
p./pp.	page(s)
para./paras.	paragraph(s)
ref./refs.	reference(s)
vol./vols.	volume(s)

Unit 17   Surveys, Questionnaires and Projects

Students in humanities and social sciences at times need to undertake surveys as part of their studies. Questionnaires may be a part of the survey and the results may be incorporated in a report. This unit gives practice in constructing questionnaires and using them to gather information. It also gives practice in writing up reports after the questionnaires have been analysed. Practice in conducting surveys is also given through group projects. The Structure and Vocabulary Aid draws attention to the types of question and their purpose. It also gives advice about constructing questionnaires.

Stage 1
Survey of Views

1   Read the report below of 'A Survey of General Personal Views'. Notice the structure of the account: the introduction, paragraphing and the cautious conclusion. Notice also the verb forms used.

2   Complete the questionnaire on the next page. It can be photocopied and collected for analysis. Then write a report of the main findings for your class based on the model below.

A Survey of General Personal Views

On 15th February 1999, an instant survey was carried out among 18 overseas postgraduate students; 11 students were male and 7 were female. The purpose of the survey was to discover the views of the students on a number of matters of
5   personal concern.

The survey was conducted by means of a questionnaire given to the students to complete. There were five questions (with one exception, each involved ticking items on a list). The first question concerned favourite colour, and the second,
10   favourite number. The next three questions were all concerned with aspects of marriage: number three looked at the ideal age to get married, number four examined the qualities looked for in a partner, and number five asked about the ideal number of children.

15   The main findings were as follows. Blue was the most popular colour, chosen by 28%; this was followed by green and purple, each selected by 22% and red with 11%. No-one chose brown, orange or black. There was no real significance in the choice of a lucky number (numbers 3, 6, and 13 each
20   chosen by 11%); 33% of the students said they had none.

61% of the students selected the age group 26–30 years as ideal for marriage, followed by 21–25 years, chosen by 33%. Only one person did not believe in marriage. In looking at the most important qualities in an ideal partner, 56% wanted the
25   person to be intelligent, 39% chose natural, 33% selected loving, while 28% indicated attractive and honest. No-one chose homely, passionate, generous or serious. The ideal

QUESTIONNAIRE
A Survey of General Personal Views

1 Tick the colour you like best from those listed below.

☐ red   ☐ blue
☐ brown   ☐ grey
☐ orange   ☐ green
☐ yellow   ☐ purple
☐ white   ☐ black

2 Which is your lucky or favourite number? _____
   (if you do not have one, write *none*)

3 What do you consider to be the ideal age to get married? Tick
   one of the age groups below.

☐ 16–20 years   ☐ 31–35 years
☐ 21–25 years   ☐ 36–40 years
☐ 26–30 years   ☐ 41–45 years
If none of these, state what you think here _____

☐ Tick here if you do not believe in marriage.

4 Tick below the three most important qualities you would look
   for in your ideal partner.

☐ lively   ☐ hard-working   ☐ confident
☐ cheerful   ☐ ambitious   ☐ generous
☐ attractive   ☐ natural   ☐ humorous
☐ intelligent   ☐ kind   ☐ serious
☐ honest   ☐ passionate   ☐ reliable
☐ thrifty   ☐ loving   ☐ faithful
☐ homely   ☐ romantic

5 What do you consider to be the ideal number of children in a
   marriage? Tick one of the following.
☐ 0   ☐ 4
☐ 1   ☐ 5
☐ 2   ☐ more than 5
☐ 3

Are there any other categories and/or questions that you
would like to add to the questionnaire? Discuss with a partner
and when agreement has been reached add the items below.

number of children was 2, chosen by 56%, followed by 3,
selected by 17%, and 1 chosen by 11%. 4 or more than 5
30 children were each selected by 1 student, while no-one
indicated no children.

It is not easy to reach any definite conclusions based upon
such a small sample of students from such widely differing
backgrounds. However, some general comments can be
35 made. The three most popular colours, in order, were blue,
green and purple. One third of the students had no lucky
numbers and no particular number was chosen by a majority
of students. It was clear that a majority favour 26–30 as the
ideal age to get married with an intelligent partner and
40 produce two children.

Stage 2
Survey of Facts

1 Read this report of a survey of the reading habits of students. Then
read the instructions that follow.

Survey of Academic and General Reading in English

On 8th February 1999, a survey was conducted among 16
overseas postgraduate students at the University of England.
The purpose of the survey was to discover the reading habits
in English of the students.
5   The survey was conducted by means of a questionnaire
given to the students to complete. The first part of the
questionnaire dealt with the type of reading and its frequency.
The second section was concerned with newspapers: the type
of items read and those that were read first.
10   From the table of data, the most significant items are as
follows. In the first section 81% of the students regularly read
academic books, while 44% regularly read academic journals.
Nothing else is read regularly or often by 40% or more of the
students. The following comments can be made about the
15 reading of newspapers, magazines and fiction. 75%
sometimes read regional or local newspapers, 69% sometimes
read books of fiction, 62% sometimes read general magazines,
and 56% sometimes read national daily newspapers. On the
other hand, 37% never read Sunday newspapers and 31%
20 never read fiction.

In the second section, not surprisingly, 100% read news
about their own country in newspapers and 56% read this
first. 94% read international news, 25% read this first. 81%
read about Britain and look at radio and TV information. The
25 only other item that is usually read by more than 50% of the
students is current affairs (read by 56%).

If any conclusions may be drawn from the data, they are,
perhaps, as follows. Overseas students presumably have little
time for general reading: most of their reading time is spent on
30 books and journals on their own subject. Outside their studies,
apart from reading news about their own country, international
news, and news about Britain, they probably spend most time
watching TV and listening to the radio.

2 Complete the questionnaire, 'Survey of Students' use of Study Time' on the next page as part of a survey of the number of hours you and other students in your class or group spend studying.

3 When the questionnaire has been completed, analyse the results and write an account of the main findings as follows.

Paragraph 1: Introduction

Paragraph 2: Breakdown into sex, age, disciplines

Paragraph 3: Analysis of the total

Paragraph 4: Main differences between disciplines

Paragraph 5: Aspects that you found unusual, unexpected, or interesting; how you compared with the average

Paragraph 6: Main conclusions

4 Are there any changes you would like to make to the questionnaire? Discuss.

Pyramid Discussion
Organising Studies

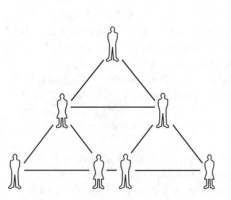

1 Select the three most important considerations that will ensure that you benefit most from your studies from the list below. The order of choices is not important.

1 drawing up a personal timetable
2 arranging time every day for private study
3 having sufficient sleep every night
4 restricting social life
5 being punctual for classes/lectures/tutorials
6 not leaving essays etc. until the last moment
7 developing a study routine and keeping to it
8 organising a system for keeping notes and references
9 borrowing books from the library as soon as they are needed
10 eating regularly and adequately
11 knowing how long it takes you to read books/journals
12 being realistic about your use of time
13 ensuring that you relax at least one day a week
14 having alternative interests to keep you fresh
15 planning each day in detail
16 working in a quiet environment
17 having an adequate supply of stationery e.g. files, notebooks
18 taking regular exercise or playing sports

Finally, add some strategies of your own that are not included in the list above.

2 With a partner devise a questionnaire on Organising Studies so that it will elicit information and views about the items listed above.

QUESTIONNAIRE
Survey of Students' Use of Study Time

Table 1 Studying: subject, level, type

(tick one box in each group)

a   ☐ arts/humanities   ☐ social sciences
       ☐ science, technology,   ☐ interdisciplinary
         medicine

b   ☐ undergraduate   ☐ postgraduate
       ☐ other

c   ☐ course   ☐ research
       ☐ other

Table 2: Sex and age

a   circle appropriately: male / female

b   tick appropriate age band:
       ☐ 15–20   ☐ 31–35
       ☐ 21–25   ☐ 36–40
       ☐ 26–30   ☐ 41+

Table 3: Hours spent in studying

	Number of hours per day (average or typical)		TOTAL per day
	timetabled work*	informal study**	
Monday			
Tuesday			
Wednesday			
Thursday			
Friday			
Saturday			
Sunday			
TOTAL per week			GRAND TOTAL per week

*   e.g. lectures, seminars, tutorials, supervisions, laboratory classes
** e.g. library use, private study, research

Stage 3
Group Projects

Group projects can be a kind of mini-research exercise. You can divide yourselves into small groups (perhaps 3–6) with each person responsible for one aspect or part of the activity: you will need to agree on who does what. Afterwards you will need to put all your information together and write a joint report.

Your project may contain a questionnaire that you need to construct for a specific purpose (perhaps to collect data or to obtain peoples' opinions on issues or matters of concern by means of interviews). It may involve investigating various sources of information or references, perhaps in libraries. It may also involve personal observation of certain matters and comparing these observations with other people. Finally, some kind of conclusion will need to be agreed upon.

1 In your group select one of the following projects and decide on a framework for collecting the data etc. and who will be responsible for which part.

   a facilities in your college/university for international students
   b types of student accommodation available and any problems arising
   c the library system and borrowing arrangements; suggestions for changes to benefit students
   d the main subjects studied at different levels in your college/university
   e the history and development of the college/university and/or town
   f public transport available locally and transport problems in the town
   g types of pollution and resulting problems in the town/environment
   h main types of industry, services and employment locally

With the agreement of your teacher you could modify the above topics. Together with your teacher you could propose other projects suitable for your locality.

Structure and Vocabulary Aid

A **Asking questions**

When constructing a questionnaire or interviewing someone, there are some points to consider in selecting the questions to ask:
- the purpose of the question and therefore the best type of question to use;
- the grammatical form or pattern of the question i.e. if a question word is necessary, verb and tense, and word order.

B **Main types of questions**

Yes/No questions – so called because they can be answered *Yes* or *No*. They begin with an auxiliary verb (e.g. *is, are, was, were, shall, will, do, does, did*) e.g. *Is the library open during the vacations? Yes (it is). No (it isn't).*

Question-word questions – sometimes called **wh- word questions.** They begin with: *What, Which, Where, When, Who, Whose, Why* and *How . . . ?*
e.g. *When is the library open? Every day except Sunday.*
What time does the library open? 9 o'clock.

Alternative questions – they contain *or* and normally offer a choice of alternative answers.
e.g. *Do you prefer travelling by train or (by) car?*

Note:	Questions beginning with *Why* and *How* can be very open questions (and perhaps difficult to answer); they are the type to elicit personal opinions or information, e.g. *Why do you prefer the theatre to the cinema? How long have you lived here?*

C Constructing a questionnaire

The examples of questionnaires in Stages 1 and 2 show some of the different formats often used: ticking items in lists or boxes, and writing numbers or brief information. In addition other types are often used:

– a straight choice between two answers, e.g.
Do you agree . . . ? Yes/No (or plus: *Don't know*)

– making choices on a scale, e.g.
What is your opinion of the course? Write a number on the scale 1–10 (where 1 = very poor, 5 = satisfactory, and 10 = excellent).

– open-ended questions, e.g.
What did you enjoy most about the course? (and why?)

Note:	1 Remember that open-ended questions take longer to analyse and summarise.
	2 Questionnaires need to be constructed carefully so that the questions are clear, brief and not ambiguous in any way. It is best to try a pilot version (a small-scale test) with friends to sort out any 'teething problems' (early minor problems) e.g. the wrong question for the purpose, omitted questions.

Unit 18   Proofreading

After you have produced the first draft (or rough version) of your writing and revised it, it will be necessary to proofread it before submitting it to a teacher or other academic person. This involves checking carefully the academic style and the details of grammar, spelling, punctuation and capital letters. More information about this is included in the Structure and Vocabulary Aid and in Appendix 1.

To produce the best writing it may be necessary to rewrite several drafts. In this unit some practice is given in checking and proofreading, concentrating on some of the details that frequently cause problems.

Stage 1
Grammar and Vocabulary

1   In each of the following sentences there are some errors. Most of them are grammatical but sometimes the word form or spelling is wrong. Underline the parts of the sentences that contain mistakes and write out all the sentences correctly. (Appendix 1 includes some guidance on the common types of error.)

a   Table 4 is showing that most of this accidents occurs to young childs.

b   Each worker pay a small money which is deducted of salary.

c   Specialist doctors in hospitals can divide in surgeons which operate the body and another specialists which act as consultant.

d   The schools number growed gradually untill 1965 and then number rised suddenly.

e   When a country apply for aids foreign, because it has no enough resources of own.

f   Is bigger and more better in country A as in country B.

g   In the other hand, we looks the table of informations, we will see this facts.

h   The problem were solve by introduction of machineries.

2   In each of the following sentences choose the correct word from those given in brackets and write it in an appropriate form in the space provided.

a   He _____ a big effort to finish his essay yesterday. (do/make)

b   The painting of the university was _____ by a famous artist. (do/make)

c   Last week her supervisor _____ her to prepare a talk for tomorrow. (tell/say)

d   The university _____ students' fees by 10% last year. (rise/raise)

e   The number of international students applying for entry to British universities _____ by 5% last October. (rise/raise)

3 Now choose the correct word from each pair of words in brackets and write it in the space provided.

a It is possible to _____ four books at a time from the library. (lend/borrow)

b Tutors often give good _____ (advice/advise) but students sometimes _____ (choice/choose) not to follow it.

c People often find that _____ (there/their) general attitude is _____ (affected/effected) by the _____ (whether/weather).

d The college _____ (principal/principle) said that information about the examination was _____ (eminent/imminent): it was likely to be announced in _____ (too/two) days' time.

e Of _____ (mathematics/mathematical) and _____ (politics/political), the former is, perhaps, more _____ (logic/logical) than the _____ (later/latter).

Stage 2
Spelling and Punctuation

Recognition

1 Each word in CAPITAL LETTERS is spelled correctly. Find a word on the right that is the same as the word on the left: e.g. 1C. If you do not have much difficulty with English spelling, cover the word in capital letters before you look at the words in small letters.

	A	B	C	D
1 ACCOMMODATION	acommodation	accomodation	accommodation	acomodation
2 CRITICISM	criticicm	criticism	critisism	critism
3 DEVELOPMENT	developement	divelopment	development	divelopement
4 DISAPPEARED	disapeared	dissappeared	dissapeared	disappeared
5 FOREIGNER	foreigner	foriegner	forienger	foreinger
6 HYPOTHESIS	hypophysis	hypotheses	hypothesis	hypophesis
7 KNOWLEDGE	knowlege	knowledge	knoledge	nowledge
8 NECESSARY	necessary	necesary	neccesary	neccessary
9 OCCURRED	occured	ocurred	ocured	occurred
10 REFERRING	referring	refering	reffering	refereeing
11 STUDYING	stuyding	studing	studying	istudying
12 SUCCESSFUL	succeful	successful	sucessful	successfull

Correction

2 The following 20 words are all spelled **wrongly**. Correct them.

a abscense
b accomodation
c arguement
d acheive
e critism
f dissapeared
g embarassed

h exagarated
i grammer
j greatfuly
k medecine
l millenium
m mispelled
n occured

o pronounciation
p reaserch
q refered
r sucussfull
s transfered
t withold

Identification

3 Some of the following 12 words are spelled wrongly. Identify those containing errors and write the words out correctly.

a aquired
b begining
c conceive
d consiense
e evidence
f inavation

g interesting
h proffesional
i recieved
j separated
k useful
l wether

Punctuation

4 All forms of punctuation have been omitted from the following passage. Write it out, putting in all the necessary punctuation marks and capital letters.

Academic conventions

when a student goes to study in another country some initial problems may be caused by differences in academic conventions or customs even the academic staffs titles can be confusing for example the title professor does not have exactly the same status everywhere differences can occur in english speaking countries eg uk usa canada australia new zealand in some it may mean the most senior of academics in others simply a university teacher some students may be uncertain how to use titles they may ask themselves the question how do i address a professor when i meet one do i say for example good morning professor smith

---

5 Write a brief description of some of the academic conventions of your country. Ensure that all punctuation details are correct.

Stage 3
Writing and
Proofreading

1 Write a short description of the difficulties that you have when writing in English. Divide the difficulties into different categories (grammar, spelling, etc.) and provide some examples of each type. First write the outline in note form, listing the main types. Then write the first draft of your description. Leave it for at least one day and then proofread it carefully, looking for errors in layout (paragraphs), grammar (including word order), vocabulary, spelling and punctuation. Correct your errors.

2 When you have finished correcting your writing, exchange it with another student for his/her description of difficulties. Read each other's writing, looking carefully for any mistakes that each of you may have missed.

Structure and Vocabulary Aid

A **Advice and suggestions for drafting and proofreading**

– If possible, leave the first draft for one or two days or longer before reading it again. Perhaps give it to a friend to read for comments. (What do you like best? Is anything unclear? Is anything omitted?)

– Check for the inclusion of signals to help the cohesion of the writing e.g. *Firstly, . . . then . . . next . . . after this . . . Finally, . . .*

– Remember that the longer a sentence is, the more likely it is to contain errors.

– Ensure that in any critical analysis or evaluation in the writing, facts are separate from opinions.

– When proofreading, check for all the items mentioned in Appendix 1 (e.g. wrong verb tense, wrong word form, singular/plural, etc.). A common mistake is for articles (*a/an/the*) to be omitted or used wrongly.

B **Spelling and pronunciation**

1 It is important to note that if you are using a word processor or computer for your writing, and make use of a spell-check programme, spelling mistakes can still occur. The reason for this is that such a spell-check does not identify places where a wrong word has been used (perhaps because two words are homophones – they have the same pronunciation but different spellings e.g. *their/there, too/two*)

2 Problems can be caused if you always try to write a word as you hear it: you will probably spell the word wrongly. The two lists below highlight the problem.

different **spellings** of the 'sh' sound	different **sounds** of the spelling -*ough*	
<u>sh</u>oe	tough	/tʌf/
<u>s</u>ugar	though	/ðəʊ/
is<u>s</u>ue	thought	/θɔːt/
man<u>si</u>on	thorough	/θʌrə/
mis<u>si</u>on	through	/θruː/
na<u>ti</u>on	bough	/baʊ/
suspi<u>ci</u>on	cough	/kɒf/
o<u>ce</u>an	hiccough (or: hiccup)	/hikʌp/
con<u>sci</u>ous		
ma<u>chi</u>ne		
fu<u>chs</u>ia		
<u>sch</u>edule		

3   A number of words have **silent letters**: e.g.
     b – when final after the sound /m/ e.g. *climb, comb, thumb*
        – before the sound /t/ e.g. *debt, doubt, subtle*
     g – usually in the combination *gn* in initial or final position
        e.g. *gnaw, reign, sign*
        – in the combination of letters *-ough* e.g. *though*
     h – before a strongly stressed vowel e.g. *hour, honour, honest*
        – in the combinations *kh, rh* and *gh* e.g. *khaki, rhyme, ghost*
     k – in the initial combination *kn* e.g *knife, knock, know*
     l – in a number of words before a consonant letter e.g. *half, talk, should*
     w – in the group *wr* e.g. *write, wrist, wrong*
        – in a number of words e.g. *two, answer, who*

C   Some spelling rules

1   **i** before **e** (the best known rule)

   i before **e** (e.g. *achieve*) except after **c** (e.g. *receive*), when making the long /iː/ sound

   e before **i** if other sounds are being made (e.g. /eɪ/ or /aɪ/ . . . *eight, reign, foreign, neighbour, feint, either, leisure*)

   Some exceptions: *protein, seize, weird, ancient*

2   The formation of plurals
     – Usually add *s* e.g. *book – books*
     – Whereas most nouns that end in *o* add *s* to form the plural e.g. *radio – radios*, some need *es* to form the plural e.g. *echo – echoes, hero – heroes, mosquito – mosquitoes, potato – potatoes, tomato – tomatoes*
     – Nouns which end in *ch, sh, s, ss, x, z, zz*, add *es* to form the plural e.g. *catch – catches, address – addresses*
     – Nouns which end in *y*:
       If the letter before the *y* is a consonant, change the letter *y* to *i* and add *es*, e.g. *copy – copies, family – families*
       If there is a vowel before the *y*, just add *s*, e.g. *delay – delays, key – keys*
     – Most nouns which end in *f* or *fe* add *s* to form the plural e.g. *chief – chiefs, proof – proofs, safe – safes*
       However, some nouns change *f* to *v* and add *es* to form the plural e.g. *half – halves, knife – knives, leaf – leaves, life – lives, self – selves, shelf – shelves, thief – thieves, wife – wives*

3   Suffix *full*. When adding *full* to the end of a word, use one *l*, e.g. *useful, beautiful*

4   Spelling of the sound 'seed' /siːd/
     – Only one word has *-sede* . . . *supersede*
     – Only three words have *-ceed* . . . *exceed, proceed, succeed*
     – the rest have *-cede* . . . *precede*

D British and American spellings

Consistency is needed in their use: you should not switch from one to the other. Some of the main groups of spelling differences are exemplified below.

UK	USA	UK	USA
centre	center	cheque	check
labour	labor	tyre	tire
programme	program	licence	license
to practise	to practice	jewellery	jewelry
catalogue	catalog	kerb	curb
traveller	traveler		

E Punctuation marks

The following passage shows the main punctuation marks in use.

question mark

inverted commas/quotation marks
semi-colon
capital letters
exclamation mark
apostrophe

full stop
hyphen
comma
dash
brackets
colon

"Why study English?" is the title of a book; it is also a question. An English-speaking pupil, or a student, might answer "Because I've got to!"—especially if they are at school (where it is part of the syllabus: compulsory until the age of sixteen).

comma (,)
Together with the full stop, the comma is the most commonly used punctuation mark. Basically it separates parts of a sentence.

full stop (.)
A full stop is used to end a sentence. The next sentence begins with a capital letter.

colon (:)
A colon is a rather infrequent punctuation mark. It indicates a fairly close interdependence between the units it separates.
– Basically, it indicates that what follows it is an explanation or amplification of what precedes it.
  e.g. *I have some news for you: John's father has arrived.*
– It can be used to introduce a list of items, often preceded by *namely, such as, as follows,* etc.
  e.g. *Please send the items indicated below, namely:*
  (i) passport (ii) visa application (iii) correct fee.

semi-colon (;)
- A semi-colon coordinates or joins two independent but related clauses or sentences.
  e.g. *The lecture was badly delivered; it went on far too long as well.*
- It is used in lists to show sub-groupings.
  e.g. *The chief commodities are: butter, cheese, milk, eggs; lamb, beef, veal, pork; oats, barley, rye and wheat.*

hyphen (-)
- A hyphen separates, in some cases, the prefix from the second part of the word.
  e.g. *co-opt*
- It joins some compound words.
  e.g. *self-control, twenty-one*

apostrophe (')
- An apostrophe is most frequently used to indicate genitive (possessive) singular and plural.
  e.g. *the student's, the students'*
- It is also used in contractions to indicate letters omitted.
  e.g. *I've = I have*
  didn't = did not

question mark (?)
A question mark is used after a direct question.
e.g. *What time is it?*
It is not used after an indirect question.
e.g. *Please tell me what time it is.*

dash (–)
A dash is used to indicate a break, often informally.
e.g. *He received a prize – and a certificate as well.*

quotation marks (quotes) or inverted commas: they may be single (' ') or double (" ")
They enclose the actual words of direct speech.
e.g. *He said, 'Why did you do that?'*

exclamation mark (!)
An exclamation mark is not often used. It is usually only used after real exclamations and sometimes after short commands.
e.g. *Oh dear! Get out!*

brackets (parentheses): ( )
- Brackets are used to clarify, or to avoid confusion.
  e.g. *He (Mr Brown) told him (Mr Jones) that he (Mr Green) had been accepted for the job.*
- They are also used for cross-references and some periods of time, in more formal writing.
  e.g. *William Smith (1910–1969) lived first in Manchester (see p.70) and then . . .*

F Capital letters

These are used:
- At the beginning of a sentence.
- For names of people, places, rivers, etc.
- For titles of people and names of things and places when referring to particular examples.
  e.g. a *university*, but *Cambridge University*, or the *University of Cambridge*
  e.g. *Miss Smith*, *Mrs Brown*, *Ms White*, *Dr Green*, *Mr Jones*, *Professor Williams*
- For nations and adjectives of nationality.
  e.g. the *Netherlands*, a *Dutchman*, *Dutch*
- For names of days, months, festivals, and historical eras.
  e.g *Monday*, *January*, *Christmas*, *Ramadan*, *the Middle Ages*
- For titles of books, plays, works of art, etc.
  e.g. *Animal Farm*, *Hamlet*, *the Mona Lisa*
- For many abbreviations.
  e.g. *R.S.V.P.*, *Ph.D.*

Unit 19   Examinations

Exams or tests can be divided into two basic types: objective and subjective. Objective tests usually involve either multiple-choice questions (where only one answer is correct out of several given answers) or true/false questions. In this unit we are concerned with subjective tests only: these require essay-type answers.

The practice in this unit is suitable for both internal exams (in colleges/universities) and external exams, e.g. IELTS (the International English Language Testing System from the University of Cambridge Local Examinations Syndicate, Cambridge), UETESOL (the University Entrance Test in English for Speakers of Other Languages from the Northern Examinations and Assessment Board, Manchester), and TOEFL (the Test of English as a Foreign Language from the Educational Testing Service, USA).

All subjective exams and tests that need essay-type answers require students to be able to:
– understand and carry out instructions;
– understand the different question types and answer appropriately and relevantly;
– divide the time equally between the questions;
– write fairly quickly.

Stage 1
Instructions

1 It is important to read the instructions and questions very carefully before you start to write anything in an examination. For the practice exercise below, use your notebook or a sheet of paper. Give yourself only five minutes to finish. **Read all the instructions carefully before you begin**.

a Write your full name in BLOCK CAPITALS at the top of the page, in the centre, and underline it.
b Under that, on the left, write the words **Date of birth:** and underline them.
c Next to that, write your date of birth.
d Under that, in the centre, write the letters **CV** (short for the Latin 'curriculum vitae' – a record of your education and employment). Underline CV.
e Under that, at the top left, write the heading **Education and Qualifications**.
f Now list, in date order, the schools, colleges and/or universities that you have attended.
g Next to each college/university write the qualification that you have received, together with the year.
h If you have worked at all, add the heading **Career** or **Employment** to the left.
i Under that, in date order, list any jobs that you have had, together with places and dates.
j At the bottom, to the left, sign your name and add today's date next to it.
k Now that you have finished reading the instructions, do a, b and c only.

2 Look carefully at the outline of the exam paper below, then answer the questions that follow it.

Examination Question Paper
9.45 am – 12.45 pm

ANSWER THREE QUESTIONS: Question 1 and TWO OTHERS.
AT LEAST ONE QUESTION MUST BE FROM EACH SECTION.

Section A
1.   EITHER
     (a) . . .
     OR
     (b) . . .
2.   . . .
3.   . . .
4.   . . .
5.   . . .

Section B
6.   EITHER
     (a) . . .
     OR
     (b) . . .
7.   . . .
8.   . . .
9.   . . .
10. . . .

---

a How long is the exam? _____

b How many questions must be answered?

   _____

c Are any questions compulsory? _____

d How many questions are there altogether to choose from?

   _____

e How many questions do you have to answer from Section A?

   _____

f Is it compulsory to answer Question 6? _____

g Is it possible to answer Questions 1(a) and (b)?

   _____

h Approximately how long should you spend writing each answer (maximum)? _____

Stage 2
Writing Tasks

Practice is given below in describing data and answering a discussion type of question. This type of practice is particularly appropriate for the IELTS Test in Academic Writing (total length: one hour). The glossary at the end of this unit will be generally useful for understanding the different question types found in examination and essay questions.

1 Write a report for your teacher describing the information shown below. You should spend about 20 minutes on this and write at least 150 words.

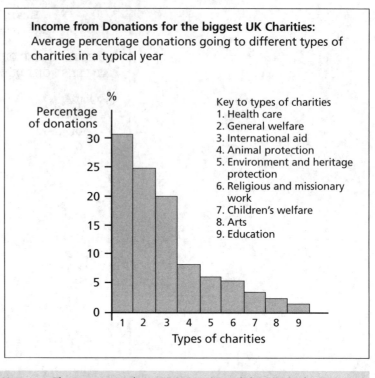

Income from Donations for the biggest UK Charities:
Average percentage donations going to different types of charities in a typical year

Percentage of donations

Key to types of charities
1. Health care
2. General welfare
3. International aid
4. Animal protection
5. Environment and heritage protection
6. Religious and missionary work
7. Children's welfare
8. Arts
9. Education

Types of charities

Note: There are more than 175,000 registered charities in the UK.

2 Present a written argument or case to an educated (non-specialist) reader on the following topic. You should spend about 40 minutes on this and write at least 250 words. You should use your own ideas and knowledge and support your arguments with examples and relevant evidence.

> In times of crisis, more and more people around the world are in need of international help. Both governments and charities provide international aid.
>
> To what extent do you think that charities should be involved in giving aid independently of governments?

In your answer describe or comment on the following:
- the situation
- the main problem
- the kinds of responses there have been or could be to the problem
- how you evaluate the responses
- your suggested solution

3 Which types of charities are the most popular in your country? What are their aims? How do people help the charities? Evaluate the work of the charities and the support they get. Can you suggest any other type of charitable work that is needed and how it could be sponsored?

Pyramid Discussion
Preparing for an Examination

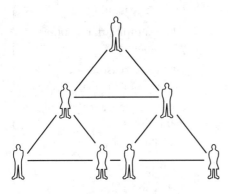

1 Select the three most important strategies for successful preparation for an examination from the list below. The order of the choices is not important.

1 Prepare a revision timetable or plan.
2 Revise regularly.
3 Analyse past exam papers and select topics for revision.
4 Write down key words of topics for revision.
5 Practise answering questions in specified time limits.
6 Ensure that you understand exam instructions.
7 Test your memory of a topic by writing notes on it.
8 Develop techniques for remembering items (e.g. mnemonics).
9 Learn to divide time equally between exam questions.
10 Check that you understand what kind of answer is expected.
11 Practise writing clearly, concisely, consistently and relevantly.
12 Ensure that you can distinguish between facts and opinions.
13 Revise actively by making notes as you read.
14 Spend most time revising the most difficult subjects.
15 Practise paraphrasing and summarising topics and texts.

Finally, add some strategies of your own that are not included in the list above.

> **Note:** Information about organising a Pyramid Discussion is given in the Guide to Using the Book.

2 The best way to prepare for an examination is to read through all your past essays and lecture notes. Write a discussion of this point of view.

Structure and Vocabulary Aid

Glossary of examination and essay questions

Research has shown that, in general, there tend to be four main tasks that are required of students when they write essays in examinations. These are to show familiarity with:
- a concept
- the relations between/among concepts
- a process
- argumentation

There is considerable variation in the question types that are used. Remember that the question words may be qualified by the words that follow, and thus the emphasis may be changed in the question. Also bear in mind that question words may have different meanings depending on the discipline in which they are used. On the next page are the most frequently used question types, together with their possible meanings. It is possible to cross-reference some of the words for additional explanations e.g. *enumerate* has the meaning *name* and *list*; *list* is then explained as *put in sequence, catalogue, mention*.

Question word	Meaning	Question word	Meaning
account for	give reasons for; explain	*explain*	make clear; give reasons for
give an account of	describe	*express*	show, describe
analyse	divide, describe, discuss, examine, explain	*identify*	point out and describe
		indicate	show, explain
assess	decide the importance and give reasons	*infer*	conclude something from facts or reasoning
calculate	estimate, determine, weigh reasons carefully	*illustrate*	give examples that support your answer
characterise	describe	*justify*	give good reasons for; explain satisfactorily
classify	arrange into groups	*list*	put in sequence; catalogue; mention
comment on	explain the importance of		
compare	describe similarities	*mention*	describe briefly
consider	think carefully about	*name*	identify
contrast	describe differences	*outline*	give a short description of the main points
criticise	discuss and point out faults		
deduce	conclude, infer	*prove*	show that something is true or certain; provide strong evidence (and examples) for
define	state precisely the meaning of; explain		
demonstrate	show clearly by giving proof or evidence	*quantify*	express or measure the amount or quantity of
describe	say what something is like	*relate*	give an account of
determine	find out something; calculate	*show*	indicate, give evidence of, make clear, demonstrate, illustrate
differentiate between	show how something is different		
discuss	consider something from different points of view, and then give your own opinion	*speculate*	form an opinion without having complete knowledge; suggest
		state	express carefully, fully and clearly
distinguish between	describe the difference between	*suggest*	mention as a possibility; state as an idea for consideration; propose
elaborate	discuss in detail, with reasons and examples		
elucidate	explain and make clear	*summarise*	give the main points of
enumerate	name and list, and explain	*to what extent (how far)*	discuss how true facts or arguments are
estimate	calculate, judge, predict		
evaluate	assess and explain	*trace*	outline and describe
examine	look at carefully; consider	*verify*	make sure that something is accurate or true; check

Note: The ten most commonly found question words in university examinations are: *Discuss, Describe, Explain, Show, Define, List, Compare/Contrast, To what extent, Outline, Evaluate.*

In addition there are four other question words that are commonly used in conjunction with other words. These are: *how, what, which, why.*

e.g
1 *How far* – to what extent
2 *What are the implications of* – the suggested or long-term results of
   What is the significance of – the meaning and importance of
   What are the procedures – the method and order of doing something; the set of actions necessary
3 *Which factors* – what are the circumstances or conditions that bring about a result
4 *Why* – for what reason; with what purpose

Look at some past examination papers for your subject. List the question types, noting in particular the ones that appear frequently. Using that as a basis, compile a glossary for your own subject area.

Appendix 1   Language Difficulties and Types of Error

The purpose of this Appendix is to examine some of the common types of error that are often made by students when writing formal or academic English. The first step is to be aware that an error has been made; the second step is to recognise or identify it; the third step is to correct it. Of course, it is far better not to make an error in the first place! If you look carefully at what follows it should help you *not* to make some of the mistakes in your writing.

Section 1
Errors and Causes

A   Some common causes of error

1   Probably the biggest cause of error is literal translation from your own language into English. If you try to translate word for word you will make mistakes.

For example, in Nepali, the sentence *John said nothing* would be rendered as (translated) *John nothing spoke*. It is easy to see that when translating into English the word order and the sentence structure could cause difficulties, and also the vocabulary.

> **Advice:**   Try to remember English sentence patterns when you read them; then use them in your writing.

2   If you write in long complex sentences, it is easier to make mistakes: the sentence becomes complicated and the subject and verb tenses may become confused.

> **Advice:**   Try to write in fairly short sentences (perhaps at most about three lines) until you are confident that there are no mistakes.

3   If you try to write English in the same way as you speak it, you will probably write in the wrong style. Spoken language is often informal. Academic writing is normally rather formal.

> **Advice:**   Try to recognise a formal style of writing and use it. Do not mix it with an informal style.

B   Some common types of error

1   Subject and verb agreement (i.e. concord); particularly singular and plural subject with the correct verb form. E.g. they *were* (**not** they *was*). (See Section 2 below.)

2   The use of *s* at the end of the third person singular, present simple tense (i.e. stem + *s*). E.g. the writer *says* (**not** the writer *say*).

3   – *This* + singular noun, *these* + plural noun;
   – *Other* and *another* differences.

4   Uncountable nouns are often wrongly used (as if they were countable nouns). E.g. *This information is useful* (**not** *These informations are useful*).

5   When the impersonal *It* or *There* subject should be used, it is often wrongly omitted. E.g. *It seems we should . . .* (**not** *Seems that we . . .*).

6   Verb tense uses are confused, particularly the present continuous (used too frequently) and present simple. E.g. *I work* in the library every day (**not** *I am working* in . . .).

7   The formation of some verb forms is not known, particularly the present passive. The formation of the past tenses of irregular verbs also causes difficulty.

8   *No* and *not* differences in negative structures.

9   The formation and use of some of the comparative and superlative forms of adjectives and adverbs are not known. (See Unit 8, and below.)

10   The correct use of   – some prepositions: (e.g. *in, on, at, for*)
                            – the articles: *a/an/the*
                            – relative pronouns: *who, which*
                            – possessive adjectives: *his, her, their*

11   Confusion over the choice of vocabulary, e.g. *make* and *do*. The choice of synonyms will often depend on usage (or context) as much as on meaning. (See Section 4 below.)

12   Spelling mistakes. (See Unit 18.)

C   Practice in areas of language difficulty

1   Each time you do an exercise and practise the language you should be as accurate as possible: copy carefully.

2   If you make a mistake, learn from it. Try not to repeat an error.

3   Do not forget the seemingly simple or obvious elements of writing, e.g. write as legibly or clearly as possible. Remember, if someone cannot read your writing, it does not matter how accurate it is!

4   Check your punctuation: if you have used a full-stop (.) it indicates the end of a sentence and immediately after it the next sentence will begin with a capital letter.

5   Do **not** mix capital letters and small letters within a word: it gives the impression that you are uneducated!

6   Remember to divide your writing into paragraphs: it makes it easier to read and creates a better impression.

Section 2
Subject-Verb Concord

A The *s* is often wrongly forgotten in the 3rd person singular of the present tense, i.e. the stem + *s*, e.g. **not** The student *attend* the language course and he *study* hard. It should be *attends* and *studies*.

B Frequently *has* and *have* are used wrongly, e.g. **not** The course *have* taught me a lot. Here it should be *has*.

C Mistakes are also made with *is* and *are*, and *was* and *were*, e.g. **not** Jose and Eduardo *is* from Mexico; **not** Some students *was* late this morning. It should be *are* and *were*.

D Another common mistake is with *do* and *does*, especially in negative sentences, e.g. **not** He *don't* study Chemistry, he *study* Physics. It should be *doesn't* (or *does not*) *study* and *studies*.

You must be careful to look at the subject of the verb, decide if it is singular or plural and then choose the appropriate verb form: Stem + *s*, *has*, *is*, *was* or *does*, if singular (all end in *s*). Stem, *have*, *are*, *were* or *do*, if plural.

Other points to note

E Look at this sentence:
The number of students on the course is less than last year.
Here the subject is *the number of students on the course* but the main word is *number*. Therefore the verb must be singular *is*. Often a mistake is made by using the plural verb (*are* in this case) because of the influence of a plural noun (*students*).

F Some nouns which are grammatically singular may be followed by a plural verb form. These are often called collective nouns. E.g. The government *have* taken an important decision. The England football team *were* beaten by Italy. The class *have* a test on Friday.
With collective nouns in their singular form it is usually possible to use either a singular verb or a plural verb. Therefore, The government *has* taken . . . The England football team *was* beaten . . . The class *has* a test . . .

G Learn by heart these examples:
1 Almost always singular
(i.e. verb in singular form): *news, information, music, mathematics, phonetics, the United States, advice, evidence, accommodation, equipment.*
e.g The news *was* very good.
2 Usually singular
aid, research
e.g. His research *is* progressing very well.
3 Always plural
(i.e. verb in plural form): *people, police, cattle.*
e.g. The police *are* doing their best to control the traffic.

4 Singular and plural
(i.e. these words do **not** change; but the verb may be singular or plural according to the meaning): *means, series, species, sheep, aircraft.*
e.g. The series of experiments that he conducted *was* very successful.
Several species of butterfly *are* in danger of dying out.

Section 3
Comparisons

A Formation

1 The regular comparative and superlative forms of adjectives and adverbs are formed as follows:
  a by adding the endings -*er* and -*est* to words with one syllable.
  b by placing the words *more* and *most* in front of words with three or more syllables.

word length	adjective or adverb	comparative	superlative
one syllable	new soon	newer sooner	newest soonest
three syllables or more	easily convenient	more easily more convenient	most easily most convenient

  c words with two syllables may be like a or b above:
  • Generally they will add the ending -*er* and -*est* if they end in:
      -*y* or -*ly* e.g. *funny* (funni*er*, funni*est*); *friendly* (friendli*er*, friendli*est*)
      But **adverbs** ending in -*ly* take *more* and *most*.
      e.g. *quickly* (*more* quickly, *most* quickly)
      -*ow* e.g. *narrow* (narrow*er*, narrow*est*)
      -*le* e.g. *able* (abl*er*, abl*est*)
      -*er* e.g. *clever* (clever*er*, clever*est*)
  • Most of the remaining words take *more* and *most*:
      e.g. careful (*more* careful, *most* careful)
  • Some common two-syllable adjectives can have either type of comparison: common, handsome, polite, quiet.
      e.g. polite   polit*er*   polit*est*
              more polite   *most* polite

2 Irregular comparison is made by:
  a a small group of very frequent adjectives:
      e.g. bad   *worse*   *worst*
             far   *further/farther* *furthest/farthest*
             good   *better*   *best*
             many   *more*   *most*
  b a small group of adverbs:
      e.g. badly   *worse*   *worst*
             little   *less*   *least*
             much   *more*   *most*

B Use in sentence construction

There are a number of constructions using comparisons. Some of the commonest ones are shown below in sentences:

1 Showing **equivalence** (i.e. the same)
   a Ann is *as* clever *as* Tom.
   b This book is *the same* price *as* that one.
   c There are *as many* students in this room *as* in the other one.
   d There is *as much* liquid in the first test-tube *as* in the second.

2 Showing **non-equivalence** (i.e. not the same)
   a The medical library is *not as/so* big *as* the science library.
   b John's essay was long*er than* Peter's.
   c However, Peter's essay was *more* carefully written *than* John's and contained *fewer* mistakes (*than* John's).
   d There were *not as many* students in the seminar *as* at the lecture.
   e The student did *not* do *as much* homework *as* his teacher had hoped.
   f This problem is *less* difficult *than* the previous one.

3 Showing one item **compared** with a number (i.e. the superlative)
   a He scored *the* high*est* marks in the annual examination.
   b *The most* convenient time for him to see his tutor was in the early afternoon.
   c Some economists find that *the least* interesting part of their subject is statistics.

4 Showing **parallel increase** (i.e. two comparatives)
   The bigger the problem (was), *the more* interesting he found it.

Note:	A common mistake is to confuse and mix some of the constructions, producing, for example, the wrong construction *more . . . as* which should be *more . . . than*.

See the list of recommended books for further explanation and practice at the end of this Appendix.

Section 4
Vocabulary

Vocabulary is a very large subject. It really requires a book to itself; in other words a dictionary. In fact, a good monolingual English dictionary is the best book that you, as a student of English, can buy. Recommended ones, specially compiled for the student of English are listed in Unit 8. A dictionary of synonyms (or a thesaurus) can also be helpful, if used with care.

Often a wrong word is used because a wrong choice has been made between similar words or **synonyms**. The choice of synonyms will often depend on usage, or context, as much as on meaning. A good English dictionary will give examples of usage or context that will help you to choose the correct word.

Some attention is given below to a few words that frequently cause difficulty to students. Read the information and examples carefully.

A Verbs

1 *Make* and *Do*

The basic meanings are:

make: construct, produce, form, shape, create.

do: perform, carry out, act.

However, there are large lists of idiomatic expressions containing these two verbs; they can be found in the dictionaries referred to above.

Look at these examples.

Considerable progress has been *made* with the experiment.

He found that he could not *do* the research.

He *made* a number of attempts to finish the work.

She had some difficulty in *doing* her homework.

Many discoveries have been *made* this century.

2 *Rise, Arise, Raise, Increase*

rise: (intransitive, i.e. without direct object) go up, get up, go higher.

e.g. Prices continue to *rise*.

The cost of living index *rose* by 10% last year.

The sun usually *rises* at 5 a.m. in the summer.

> **Note:** *Rise* is also a noun, meaning increase.
> e.g. There was a *rise* in prices caused by a *rise* in wages.

arise: (intransitive) come into existence, appear.

e.g. A new problem has *arisen* in the college.

An unexpected difficulty *arose* when he was analysing the results.

raise: (transitive, i.e. takes a direct object) lift up, make higher, cause to rise.

e.g. Bus fares were *raised* three times last year.

The landlord said he is going to *raise* the rent.

Also – to bring up for discussion or attention.

e.g. He *raised* a new point in the seminar.

– to manage to get; obtain.

e.g. He *raised* a loan. He tried to *raise* money for a new project.

increase: (transitive and intransitive) make or become greater in size, number, degree, etc.

e.g. The Chancellor of the Exchequer *increased* the tax on petrol in his last Budget.

The population has *increased* by 200,000 to a total of 50 million.

> **Note:** 1 *Increase* can sometimes be used instead of *raise* or *rise*.
> e.g. In the above two sentences *raised* could be used in the first and *has risen* in the second.
>
> 2 *Increase* is also a noun, meaning rise. e.g. There was a steady *increase* in population.

B Pairs of words often confused

NOUN	VERB	NOUN	ADJECTIVE
practice	practise	politics	political
advice	advise	mathematics	mathematical
effect	affect	statistics	statistical
choice	choose	logic	logical
		economics	economic

ADJECTIVE	VERB
loose	lose

Note: 1 The adjective *economical* relates to saving money, not to the *economy*.

2 Two adjectives are often confused, partly because of spelling mistakes: *later* (*late, later, latest*) and *latter* (the second of two things already mentioned; contrasted with *former*, meaning the first of two).

C British words and American equivalents

Occasionally confusion can be caused by being unaware that there are some differences between British and American words. Good English learners' dictionaries give the American equivalents of the British words. Some examples are given below.

UK	USA	UK	USA
aeroplane	airplane	rubbish	garbage/trash
autumn	fall	tap	faucet
chemist's	drugstore	timetable	schedule
city/town		tin	can
centre	downtown	torch	flashlight
flat	apartment	trousers	pants
full stop	period	vest	undershirt
pavement	sidewalk	waistcoat	vest
rubber	eraser		

Section 5
Recommended Books

The following books are recommended for further explanation and practice:

Longman Dictionary of Common Errors N.D. Turton & J.B. Heaton (Longman).
Right Word Wrong Word L.G. Alexander (Longman).
An A–Z of English Grammar and Usage G. Leech (Longman).
Practical English Usage M. Swan (Oxford University Press).
English Grammar in Use R. Murphy (Cambridge University Press).
Oxford Practice Grammar J. Eastwood (Oxford University Press).
A University Grammar of English R. Quirk & S. Greenbaum (Longman).
A Communicative Grammar of English G. Leech & J. Svartvik (Longman).
An Introduction to English Grammar S. Greenbaum (Longman).
Longman Essential Activator (Longman).

Appendix 2   Connectives

The main connectives are grouped below according to the similarity of their meaning with the three basic connectives *and*, *or*, *but*. For information about their use in sentences, you should look in a good dictionary.

1 and	**A** listing	1 enumeration		
		2 addition	a reinforcement b equation	
	B transition **C** summation **D** apposition **E** result **F** inference			
2 or	**G** reformulation **H** replacement			
3 but	**I** contrast **J** concession			

---

1   and

A Listing:
  1 **Enumeration** indicates a cataloguing of what is being said. Most enumerations belong to clearly defined sets:

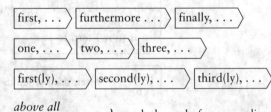

first, . . . ⟩ furthermore . . . ⟩ finally, . . . ⟩

one, . . . ⟩ two, . . . ⟩ three, . . . ⟩

first(ly), . . . ⟩ second(ly), . . . ⟩ third(ly), . . . ⟩

above all
last but not least } mark the end of an ascending order

first and foremost
first and most important(ly) } mark the beginning of a descending order

to begin/start with, . . . ⟩ in the second place, . . . ⟩ moreover, . . . ⟩ and to conclude, . . . ⟩

next, . . . ⟩ then, . . . ⟩ afterward, . . . ⟩ lastly/finally, . . . ⟩

2 **Addition,** to what has been previously indicated.

    a *Reinforcement* (includes confirmation):

> also
> again
> furthermore
> further
> moreover
> what is more
> then
> in addition
> besides
> above all
> too
> as well (as)

    b *Equation* (similarity with what has preceded):

> equally
> likewise
> similarly
> correspondingly
> in the same way

Note:

1 From the point of view of meaning the following are often the negative equivalents of *and*: *either; neither; nor; not only . . . (but) also . . .; neither . . . nor . . .*
Neither leaves the series open for further additions, whereas *nor* concludes it.

2 The truth of a previous assertion may be confirmed or contradicted by: *indeed; actually; in (actual) fact; really; in reality*

B **Transition** can lead to a new stage in the sequence of thought:

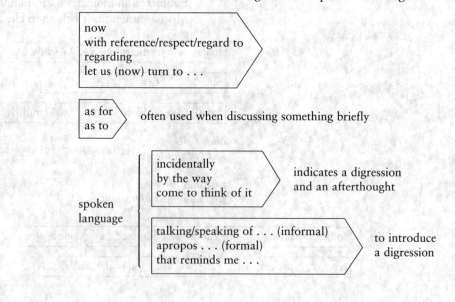

> now
> with reference/respect/regard to
> regarding
> let us (now) turn to . . .

> as for
> as to   often used when discussing something briefly

spoken language

> incidentally
> by the way
> come to think of it   indicates a digression and an afterthought

> talking/speaking of . . . (informal)
> apropos . . . (formal)
> that reminds me . . .   to introduce a digression

C **Summation** indicates a generalisation or summing-up of what has
preceded:

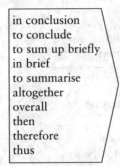

in conclusion
to conclude
to sum up briefly
in brief
to summarise
altogether
overall
then
therefore
thus

D **Apposition** is used to refer back to previous sentences or to
parallel or related references:
i.e., that is, that's to say
viz. namely
in other words
or, or rather, or better
and
as follows
e.g. for example, for instance, say, such as, including, included,
especially, particularly, in particular, notably, chiefly, mainly,
mostly (of)

The relationships that these phrases can express include:
reformulation (see 2A below), exemplification and
particularisation.

E **Result** expresses the consequence or result of what was said
before:

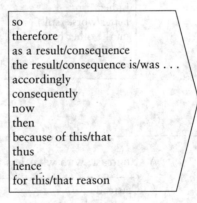

so
therefore
as a result/consequence
the result/consequence is/was . . .
accordingly
consequently
now
then
because of this/that
thus
hence
for this/that reason

F **Inference** indicates a deduction from what is implicit in the preceding sentence(s):

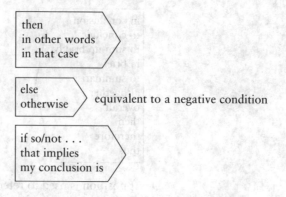

then
in other words
in that case

else
otherwise ⟩ equivalent to a negative condition

if so/not . . .
that implies
my conclusion is

---

2 or

A **Reformulation,** to express something in another way:

better
rather
in other words
in that case
to put it (more) simply

B **Replacement,** to express an alternative to what has preceded:

again
alternatively
rather
better/worse (still) . . .
on the other hand
the alternative is . . .
another possibility would be

---

3 but

A **Contrast,** with what has preceded:

instead
conversely
then
on the contrary
by (way of) contrast
in comparison
(on the one hand) . . . on the other hand . . .

B **Concession** indicates the unexpected, surprising nature of what is being said in view of what was said before:

besides	*yet*
(or) else	*in any case*
however	*at any rate*
nevertheless	*for all that*
nonetheless	*in spite of/despite that*
notwithstanding	*after all*
only	*at the same time*
still	*on the other hand*
while	*all the same*
(al)though	*even if/though*

Based upon Chapter 10: 'Sentence Connection', in *A Grammar of Contemporary English* by Quirk, Greenbaum, Leech and Svartvik (Longman).

Appendix 3   Research Reports

Students often need to write reports on their research; in an extended form these become dissertations or theses. The framework or structure of research reports is as follows.

Section 1   Basic Framework for a Research Report

Preliminaries	1	The title	The fewest words possible that adequately describe the paper.
	2	Acknowledgements	Thanking colleagues, supervisors, sponsors, etc. for their assistance.
	3	List of contents	The sections, in sequence, included in the report.
	4	List of figures/ tables	The sequence of charts or diagrams that appear in the text.
Introduction	5	The abstract	An extremely concise summary of the contents of the report, including the conclusions. It provides an overview of the whole report for the reader.
	6	Statement of the problem	A brief discussion of the nature of the research and the reasons for undertaking it. A clear declaration of proposals and hypotheses.
Main body	7	Review of the literature	A survey of selective, relevant and appropriate reading, both of primary and secondary source materials. Evidence of original and critical thought applied to books and journals.
	8	Design of the investigation	A statement and discussion of the hypotheses, and the theoretical structure in which they will be tested and examined, together with the methods used.
	9	Measurement techniques used	Detailed descriptions and discussion of testing devices used. Presentation of data supporting validity and reliability. A discussion of the analysis to be applied to the results to test the hypotheses.
	10	Results	The presentation in a logical order of information and data on which a decision can be made to accept or reject the hypotheses.
Conclusion	11	Discussion and conclusion	The presentation of principles, relationships, correlations and generalisations shown by the results. The interpretation of the results and their relationship to the research problem and hypotheses. The making of deductions and inferences, and the implications for the research. The making of recommendations.
	12	Summary of conclusions	A concise account of the main findings, and the inferences drawn from them.
Extras	13	Bibliography	An accurate listing in strict alphabetical order of all the sources cited in the text.
	14	Appendices	A compilation of important data and explanatory and illustrative material, placed outside the main body of the text.

Note: 1 There may be slight variations to the above. For example, the abstract may be separate and appear at the very beginning of the report. In its place there may be a section entitled 'Outline of the research'. 9 may be called 'Methods and procedures'. 11 may include 'Recommendations and suggestions for further research'.

2 In abbreviated form, the traditional structure of a scientific or technical report is **IMRAD** = **I**ntroduction, **M**ethods, **R**esults and **D**iscussion.

Section 2
Headings, Sub-headings and Numbering

The sections and sub-sections of reports are usually headed and numbered according to the decimal numbering system. Notice how the numbering is used below together with indentation (starting writing further away from the left margin). e.g.

5. SECTION HEADING (bold or underlined)

5.1 Sub-section heading (often underlined)

    5.2.1. sub-section

    5.2.2. sub-section

    5.2.3. sub-section

Note:	It is best not to use more than a total of three decimal numbers in the sections otherwise it becomes too complicated to read. Not every paragraph is numbered – just sections or sub-sections. Lists within a sub-section can be numbered simply: e.g. 1. 2. 3.

Section 3
Checklists

When writing any kind of report it is important that none of the items, contents or procedures are forgotten and omitted. To help in this, a checklist of the details needed is extremely useful: they can be referred to and ticked off as they are covered or included. Some of the kinds of items to include are as follows:

– the aim of the report

– collecting information/data

– noting all references

– analysis of questionnaires

– organising the information

– providing appropriate diagrams and tables

– layout of the report

Appendix 4   Correcting Code

The following is a list of suggested abbreviations and symbols to use when checking students' writing. They can be written in the margin next to the line containing the error. If you need/wish to give more help, the mistake can also be underlined.

Abbreviations

A	Article error (wrong choice or usage)
Adj.	Adjective error (wrong choice, formation or position, or omission)
Adv.	Adverb error (wrong choice, formation or position, or omission)
Cap.	Capital letter(s) needed
Gram.	Grammatical error(s) – miscellaneous e.g. countable/uncountable nouns, pronouns, negatives, connectives
P	Punctuation error
Prep.	Preposition error (wrong choice or usage)
Ref.	Reference omitted
Sp.	Spelling mistake
Str.	Structure of the sentence is wrong e.g. subject or verb omitted
SV	Subject-verb agreement/concord needed
Vb.	Wrong verb tense or verb form
Vocab.	Wrong choice of words
WO	Wrong word order

Symbols

✓   right

✗   wrong

⌃   something omitted

( )   the word(s) in brackets should be omitted

⌐   a paragraph is needed

?| meaning unclear: it needs to be rewritten

For students

If you need to request help with your writing, you could use a **help code** (you would need to discuss this with your teacher). For example, you could underline the parts of your writing that you are dissatisfied with or had difficulty with. If you are uncertain about, for example, the vocabulary or expressions or sentence construction, you could put a question mark (?) in the margin opposite the item.

Note: The above abbreviations and symbols are suggestions. They can be changed or added to depending on your needs. It is important that they are used consistently otherwise they may cause confusion.

Appendix 5   Optional Questionnaire

Your Writing and this Book

This questionnaire is for your use if your teacher would like some feedback on your progress with writing and the use you have made of this book. Answer the following questions after thinking carefully about your ability at academic writing.

1   Do you think your writing in English has improved at all during this course? YES/NO.
   – If the answer is YES, what improvements do you think you have made?

   _____

   _____

   _____

   – If the answer is NO, what do you think are the reasons?

   _____

   _____

   _____

   _____

2   What difficulties do you still have with academic writing?

   _____

   _____

   _____

3   What kind of writing practice do you think would be most useful for you now?

   _____

   _____

   _____

4   Which units in the book did you find most useful? Give the numbers.

   _____

5   How relevant and useful has this book been in helping you improve your writing
   (please tick one)

   ☐ very   ☐ reasonably   ☐ a little   ☐ not very   ☐ not at all

6   Have you any final comments to make, either about your own writing or the book?

   _____

   _____

   _____

Key to Exercises and Notes

Answers are given where the choice is restricted. Where the exercise is 'open' and there are several possible answers, a suggested answer is given.

Unit 1   Key

Answers to the Exercises

Stage 2

1 A choice of connectives from the list is possible, though *hence* is less frequently used.
  a As a result, not many read one regularly.
  b Consequently, they usually read the international news first in the newspapers.
  c Therefore, it is useful to be able to answer questions briefly.
  Suggested answers:
  d . . . not many students were able to take notes.
  e . . . it took him a long time to finish reading the English textbook.

2 A choice of connectives from the list is possible, though *in other words* is the most frequently used.
  a In other words, she is taking a long time to improve her English.
  b It would be better to say she has little difficulty in learning English.
  c In other words, she speaks it excellently.

Suggested answers:
d . . . she speaks English and French equally well.
e . . . if you have a sensitive 'ear' (or are sensitive to sound changes) you will learn languages easily.

3 A choice of connectives from the list is possible, though *however* is the most frequently used.
  a Nevertheless, Ali managed to answer them satisfactorily.
  b However, Abdul was able to obtain a grant.
  c In spite of that, Juan succeeded in completing it in time.
  Suggested answers:
  d . . . to everyone's surprise, he passed it easily.
  e . . . he insisted on continuing (with) it and completing it.

Stage 3

1 The first one, beginning: 'Each language function consists of sentences . . .'
2 1c: 'Academic writing . . .'   2a   3e   4d   5b

Unit 2   Key

Notes on the Exercises

Stage 1

1 and 4   *to* can have the meaning of *in order to*. E.g. . . . *to* whiten it; . . . *to* flatten it; . . . *to* soften it.

Stage 2

For practice in using tables and language that comments on significant items within the tables, see Unit 11: Interpretation of Data.
1 The plural of *thesis* is *theses*; we can write *The* University *of* X, or X University; *of an* average *frequency of* X per term can also be expressed as *on* average X per term.
    The percentages in the chart total more than 100% because some students did more than one type of writing.
    Phrases such as: *the majority, just over half/50%, about one-third, less than a quarter* can be used or practised in relation to the table.

Answers to the Exercises

Stage 1

2 The following verbs should be underlined: is stripped . . . are sawn . . . are conveyed . . . are placed . . . are cut . . . are mixed . . . are heated . . . crushed . . . is cleaned . . . is bleached . . . is passed . . . are produced . . . is removed . . . are pressed, dried . . . refined . . . is produced

3 are placed . . . are cut . . . which are mixed with
. . . are heated and crushed . . . which is cleaned
. . . is . . . bleached . . . is passed . . . are
produced . . . is removed . . . which are pressed,
dried and refined . . . is produced

4 c – h – a – f – e – b – d – g

5 d Glass *is made* from sand, limestone and soda
ash.

h *First*, these three minerals *are mixed* together
in the right proportions.

b *Then*, sometimes broken glass *is added*.

g *Next*, this mixture *is heated* strongly in a
furnace.

f *Then*, glass *is produced*.

a *After this*, it *is shaped* into bottles in the
mould.

c *Next*, the bottles *are reheated and cooled* to
strengthen the glass.

e *Finally*, they are ready *to be used*.

Note that a choice of sequence markers is
possible: See Appendix 2: Connectives, Section 1a.

Flow chart

1 sand 2 limestone 3 soda ash 4 broken
glass 5 a furnace 6 the mould

Stage 2

1 A survey was conducted among *50* overseas
postgraduate students at *Manchester University*
(or: *the University of Manchester*). The purpose
of the survey was to discover the type, *frequency*
and *length* of academic writing that was
expected of the students by their supervisors or
tutors. *34%* of the students *wrote* reports, of an
average frequency of two per term, *of an* average
length *of 4000 words*.

2 a was carried out b were distributed c were
requested d were collected e were analysed
f were published

Stage 3

2
a Think	j Look	s Revise
b Understand	k Decide	t Write
c Make	l Select	u Make
d Note	m Divide	v Remember
e Add	n Write	w Compile
f Read	o Write	x Ensure
g Write	p Avoid	y Add
h Keep	q Read	
i Acknowledge	r Ask	

3 Suggested answer:

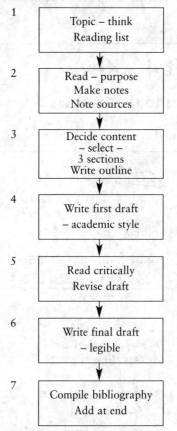

1 Topic – think
   Reading list

2 Read – purpose
   Make notes
   Note sources

3 Decide content
   – select –
   3 sections
   Write outline

4 Write first draft
   – academic style

5 Read critically
   Revise draft

6 Write final draft
   – legible

7 Compile bibliography
   Add at end

Unit 3 Key

Answers to the Exercises

Stage 1

1 1 The Atlantic Ocean 2 Scotland 3 Northern
Ireland 4 The Irish Republic (or: The Republic
of Ireland) 5 The North Sea 6 Wales
7 England 8 London 9 The English Channel
10 France

2 Alternatives are given in brackets:
(1) is surrounded by (2) comprises (consists of;
is composed of) (3) lies off (4) consists of (is
composed of; comprises) (5) is composed of
(consists of; comprises) (6) is situated in (is
located in) (7) was (8) was (is) (9) is (10) is
spoken by (11) speak

Stage 2

1 Many answers are possible; this is an example:
Australia
Australia is an extremely large island; in fact, it
is really a continent, and it lies on the Tropic of

Capricorn. To the north of it are Indonesia and Papua New Guinea, and to the south-east is New Zealand. It is surrounded by the Indian, Southern and South Pacific Oceans. It comprises eight states and territories. The capital is Canberra, which is situated in south-east Australia.

Australia has a total area of 7,682,300 square kilometres. About 7% of the land is arable, 14% is covered in forest, 54% is grassland and 25% is desert, mountains and wasteland. The country consists largely of plains and plateaux.

The climate ranges from alpine to tropical, with a wide range of rainfall. There is little or no rain in two-thirds of the country, while over 80 centimetres fall annually in the north, and the eastern and southern highlands.

In 1996 the population of Australia was 18,423,000. The density of population was an average of two people per square kilometre. More than half of the population lives in the south-eastern part of the country. English is the main language and Christianity is the main religion.

Unit 4   Key

Answers to the Exercises
Stage 1
2   Suggested notes:

```
Eng. Dicts.

From 1604 → 'hard words'/A-z
        ↓
    N. Bailey - 1721
        ↓
   Sam Johnson - 1755
"A Dict. of the Eng. Lang."
     100,000 quotes
        ↓
   U.S.A.  - 1828
   Noah Webster
    (spelling)
        ↓
  "O.E.D." - 1928
   (from 1879)
12 vols. - ½ mill. words.
```

Stage 2
1   **The United Nations**
The *origins* of the UN can *be* traced back *to* the League of Nations. This *was* an international *organisation* which *was* created *by* the Treaty of Versailles *in* 1920 with the purpose *of* achieving world peace. Before 1930, the League, from its Geneva headquarters, *organised* international conferences and did useful humanitarian work. *However*, it failed *to* deal effectively *with* international aggression *during* the 1930s. The League *was* formally closed *in* 1946 and *was* superseded *by* the United Nations.

The UN was *founded* on 24th October 1945, when the UN Charter *was* ratified *by* the 51 founder member countries. Almost *all* the countries of the *world* are now members: 185 in all.

The UN was *established* to maintain international peace, and to encourage international co-operation to overcome economic, social, cultural and humanitarian problems. Apart *from* the *principal* organs of the UN (The General Assembly, The Security Council etc.), *most* of the UN's work is done *through* its specialised bodies *and* agencies. *Some* of the best *known* are, perhaps, the FAO, ILO, IMF, WHO, UNESCO and UNICEF.

Stage 3
2   1d 2j 3g 4i 5c 6f 7a 8b 9h 10e
3   Suggested notes:

```
UNIVS. IN ENGLAND

Oldest: Oxford 1185
    ↓       Cambridge 1209
  London  1836
    ↓
C.19k/20k - civic univs. industrial areas
             (eg Manchester 1880, Birmingham 1900)
1940s/50s  - other civic univs.
    ↓        (eg Nottingham 1948)
  1960s     largest expan. of univs. - countryside
    ↓        (eg Warwick 1965)
  1969      Open Univ.
    ↓
  1992      Ed. Act - polys = univs. (total 86)
            (N.B. Buck = only ind. univ, 1983)
```

Unit 5 Key

Notes on the Exercises

When giving an extended definition of a subject it may be necessary to comment on some of the methods, processes, techniques, stages, steps, etc., involved, e.g. Moulding is one of the methods of shaping plastics. Polymerisation is the process of turning chemicals into plastics.

Notice that the form *of*+verb+*ing* is used here instead of the wh- word.

The biggest difficulty in writing a definition is to have a clear idea of the concept to be defined. This involves careful organisation of the necessary information. Finally, the language used to express the concept must be correctly selected.

In definitions it is often useful to give examples. This is the subject of Unit 6.

Answers to the Exercises

Stage 1
1   a   is an institution where   d   is an animal which
    b   is a person who   e   is a person who
    c   is a metal which   f   is a place where
2   1e . . . a person who designs . . .
    2h . . . an instrument which makes . . .
    3a . . . a machine which produces . . .
    4g . . . a person who studies . . .
    5j . . . a geometric figure which has . . .
    6i . . . a vegetable which is . . .
    7b . . . a person who studies . . .
    8f . . . a book which gives . . .
3   a3   b1 (and perhaps 3)   c2
4   Suggested answers:
    a   A lecturer is a person who teaches students in a college or university.
    b   A dictionary is a book which explains the words of a language and is arranged in alphabetical order.
    c   A degree is an academic qualification which is given by a university to a student who has passed the appropriate examinations.

Stage 2
1   a   Plastics are substances which are moulded into shape when they are heated.
    b   A mineral is a structurally homogeneous solid of definite chemical composition which is formed by the inorganic process of nature.
    c   Rayons are man-made fibres produced from wood.
    d   A fossil is an organic trace buried by natural processes and subsequently permanently preserved.
2   a   Demography is the study of population growth and its structure.
    b   Zoology is the science of the structure, forms and distribution of animals.
    c   Biology is the science of the physical life of animals and plants.
3   a   Sociology may be defined as the science which studies the nature and growth of society and social behaviour.
    b   Theology may be defined as the study of religious beliefs and theories.
    c   Astronomy may be defined as the science of the sun, moon, stars and planets.

Stage 3
1   a   Criminal psychology may be defined as the branch of psychology which investigates the psychology of crime and of the criminal.
    b   Chemistry may be defined as the branch of science which deals with the composition and behaviour of substances.
    c   Social economics may be defined as the branch of economics which is concerned with the measurement, causes and consequences of social problems.

Unit 6 Key

Notes on the exercises

Note the difference between the following abbreviations which are sometimes confused:

e.g. = for example (some examples from a list are given)
i.e. = that is (to say); in other words
    e.g. *males i.e. men and boys* . . .

viz. = namely; it is/they are
    e.g. *There are four language skills, viz. listening, speaking, reading and writing.*

Description, definition and exemplification are closely linked. So also is classification: this is in Unit 7.

Stage 1

1   There are several ways of referring to examples, not just the expression *for example* or *e.g.* (although these are the most common).

    It is safer not to use *as* or *like* as they can easily be used wrongly.

    Notice the use of the colon (:) and the comma (,) in listing examples.

Stage 2

1   When using *such as* (or the alternative forms) be careful to give only examples and not the complete set, group or list. For example, if we agree that there are four language skills (listening, speaking, reading, writing) then the following sentence would be wrong.

    The language skills, for example listening, speaking, reading and writing, need to be practised. WRONG

    However, it would be correct to put:

    The language skills, for example speaking and writing, need to be practised.

Stage 3

1   Be careful not to use *for example* or *such as* wrongly. It would be wrong to say: *There are two main kinds of writing system, for example, ideographic and phonetic* . . . because the total number is two and here *for example* lists all of them instead of only one.

Answers to the Exercises

Stage 1

1   **What is language?**
    A language is a signalling system which operates with symbolic vocal sounds, and which is used by a group of people for the purposes of communication.

    Let us look at this definition in more detail because it is language, more than anything else, that distinguishes man from the rest of the animal world.

    Other animals, it is true, communicate with one another by means of cries: for example, many birds utter warning calls at the approach of danger; apes utter different cries, such as expressions of anger, fear and pleasure. But these various means of communication differ in important ways from human language. For instance, animals' cries are not articulate. This means, basically, that they lack structure. They lack, for example, the kind of structure given by the contrast between vowels and consonants. They also lack the kind of structure that enables us to divide a human utterance into words.

    We can change an utterance by replacing one word in it by another: a good illustration of this is a soldier who can say, e.g. 'tanks approaching from the north', or he can change one word and say 'aircraft approaching from the north' or 'tanks approaching from the west'; but a bird has a single alarm cry which means 'danger!'

    This is why the number of signals that an animal can make is very limited: the great tit is a case in point; it has about twenty different calls, whereas in human language the number of possible utterances is infinite. It also explains why animal cries are very general in meaning.

2   a an example   b such as   c for instance/for example   d for example/for instance   e illustration   f a case in point

Stage 2

In these exercises different choices of language are possible.

1   a   1 There are a number of languages which are descended from Latin: for example, Provençal and Catalan.
        2 There are a number of languages, such as Provençal and Catalan, which are descended from Latin.

    b   1 There are a number of languages which are descended from Sanskrit: for example, Bengali and Hindi.
        2 There are a number of languages, such as Bengali and Hindi, which are descended from Sanskrit.

2   a   An example of such a family is the Germanic group of languages. Examples of members of the family are English and German.

    b   An example of such a family is the Sino-Tibetan group of languages. Examples of members of the family are Thai and Chinese.

Stage 3

1   Suggested answer:
    Writing may be defined as a (the) method of human intercommunication by means of conventional visible marks. There are two main kinds of writing system: firstly, ideographic, in which one sign represents one word, for example, Chinese. Secondly, phonetic: this is sub-divided into syllabic and alphabetic. In syllabic, one sign represents one syllable: examples are Amharic and Japanese kana. In alphabetic, one sign represents one sound: Greek and Arabic are examples of this system.

Unit 7   Key

Notes on the Exercises
Stage 1
Note these useful phrases:

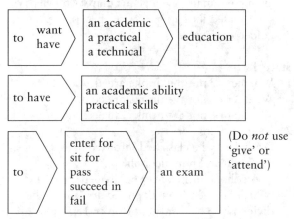

We *divide* something *into* (**not** *to*) two or more parts; note the spelling of *grammar*; the plural of *criterion* is *criteria*.

The plural of *genus* is *genera*.

Stage 2
Species is the same form for singular and plural. In the singular it can be used like this: *A species is . . .*

It is not necessary to fully understand the technical vocabulary for describing birds: it is more important to be able to use the general language of classification.

Stage 3
1   It is important to remember that in order to classify there must be clearly recognisable criteria (e.g. age, size, number of employees).
2   The criteria being used in the classification may be stated at the very beginning, as the choice of criteria determines which items are placed in which group, class etc. This may be done in a simple way, e.g.
   X may be classified according to Y (Y = the criterion)
or in a more complex way, e.g.
   In classifying industrial enterprises by size, various criteria may be used. One is the amount of fixed assets, another the value of annual production and a third the number of employees. Each of these criteria of classification has some advantages and some drawbacks . . . (Then a discussion with examples follows.)

(From 'Small Industry in the Underdeveloped Countries' by B.F. Hoselitz, in Economic Policy for Development, edited by I. Livingstone, Penguin 1971)

If more practice is needed in classifying items, or if a discussion or a group writing task are required, the following subjects might be used: animals, trees, transport, vehicles, energy, heat, newspapers, sports or games.

Answers to the Exercises
Stage 1
1   a . . . can/may be classified according to . . .
   b . . . two types of . . .
   c . . . can/may be subdivided . . .
   d . . . may be grouped according to . . .
   e . . . an examination (at 11 years).
2   1e 2b 3g 4a 5f 6d 7c
3

Diagram 1: State Schools in England and Wales

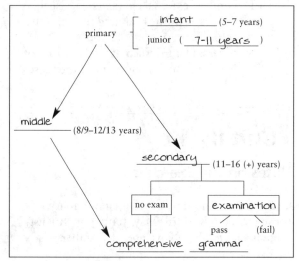

4   Suggested answer:
There are two types of school: primary and secondary. Primary schools can be sub-divided, according to age, into infant schools and junior schools. Infant schools cater for children aged 5–7 and junior schools for children aged 7–11.

Secondary schools are for children 11–16+ years and may be grouped according to whether or not an exam is taken at the age of 11. If there is no exam, children proceed to a comprehensive school. If there is an exam, children proceed to a grammar school or another secondary school, depending on their results in the exam.

Stage 2

1 *Diagram 2: The Classification of Birds*

Classification divisions or categories	Example of classification of Golden Eagle (in English) for each division	Number of the divisions
Order	Falcon-like	27
Family	Falcon	215
Genus	Eagle	–
Species	Golden Eagle	8514

2 a A bird is a creature or animal which has two wings, feathers, two legs, a toothless bill, warm blood, and can lay eggs. It is usually able to fly.

b A species is an interbreeding group of birds which do not normally mate with other such groups.

c 1 If the feet are designed so that they can grip a perch.

2 If they are song-birds.

d Sparrows and crows.

e 1 families: external characteristics such as the shape of the beak and feet, and the colour pattern of the feathers.

2 orders: features such as the structure of the skull, the arrangement of the muscles in the legs, and the condition of the young at the time of hatching.

3 There are 27 main orders of birds, for example, falcon-like birds. Each order may be divided into families, such as falcons, and each family may be sub-divided into genera: eagles are an example. Finally, each genus may be further sub-divided into a number of species, e.g. golden eagle.

Stage 3

1 Whether or not the drinks are alcoholic.
Whether or not the drinks are cold.
Whether or not the drinks are aerated.

2 Suggested answer:

Drinks may be classified into two main groups: alcoholic and non-alcoholic.

Alcoholic drinks may be divided into spirits, wine, and beer. Non-alcoholic drinks may be divided into hot and cold drinks. Examples of hot drinks are tea, coffee, and cocoa. Cold drinks may be grouped according to whether or not they are aerated. Lemonade, tonic water, soda water and Coca-Cola are examples of aerated drinks. Non-aerated drinks may be (sub-)divided into squashes, fruit juices and others.

Unit 8   Key

Notes on the Exercises

Stage 1

In Table 2 the months, in order, are: January, February, March, April, May, June, July, August, September, October, November, December.

Stage 2

1 A common error in using comparative forms is to confuse some of the items, e.g. *more . . . than* is sometimes confused with *as much as* and the wrong form *more . . . as* is produced.

Care should also be taken not to confuse other items, e.g.

(a lot) more people a lot of people	do **not** write *a lot of more people*

2 The letter might start:

Thank you for your letter of (date) in which you ask for some information about English dictionaries.

The recommendation might take these forms:

I recommend you to buy X . . .
In my opinion, Y is the book to buy . . .
If I were you I would buy Z . . .
I would advise you to buy X . . .

The letter might conclude:

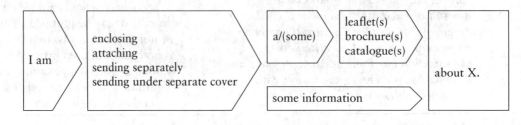

and to a friend it might end:

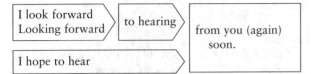

Stage 3

Generally, this stage provides some practice in using connectives, especially when contrasting items. It is important that unrelated items should not be contrasted, e.g. do **not** compare *area* and *religion*.

Answers to the Exercises

Stage 1

1 a longer than
  b not so/not nearly as . . . as
  c the longest
  d shorter than/not so long as
  e the longest
  f colder . . . than

g warmer/hotter/ wetter . . . than
h more . . . than
i most . . . the wettest
j not so/nearly as . . . as
k the driest/the coldest
l the same as/as low as
m as . . . as   n less than
o hottest/wettest . . . the wettest/hottest

Stage 2

1 a more . . . than
  b greater . . . than
  c as many . . . as
  d most
  e The same . . . as
  f least
  g Not so many . . . as
  h as much . . . as
  i More . . . than
  j biggest

  Other answers would be possible without the instruction to 'use each word only once'.

2 Various replies are possible but they will probably include reference to:
  more/fewer: words, examples, pages, appendices; bigger/smaller; higher/lower levels.

Unit 9   Key

Notes on the Exercises

It is not possible here to practise all the combinations of connectives and constructions: there are a large number for all the cause-effect relationships. The Structure and Vocabulary Aid illustrates some of the main ones.

It may be useful to remember that the following questions relate to cause-effect relations:

What caused X?
What was the effect of X?
Why did Y happen?

In Stage 2, **2** and **3** notice the difference in use between e.g. cross*ing* and cross*ed*.

Answers to the Exercises

Stage 1

1 1d 2i 3g 4f 5h 6c
2 A variety of connectives are possible. Check carefully with the Structure and Vocabulary Aid to see if particular connectives etc. fit into the particular patterns shown here. Suggested answers:

a ⬚Because⬚ he worked hard <u>he passed his examination</u>.
b Prolonged illness is often ⬚caused by⬚ <u>delayed treatment</u>.
c The strike was ⬚caused by⬚ <u>bad labour relations</u>.

d The laboratory specimens were killed ⬚as a result of⬚ <u>the fluctuation in temperature</u>.
e That bottle must be handled very carefully ⬚as⬚ <u>there is acid in it</u>.

Stage 2

1 Table 1: Climate

Cause	Connective or Marker	Effect
rising temperatures	have been causing	2 the snowline to retreat on mountains all over the world. e.g. In Peru it has risen as much as 2,700 feet in 60 years.
—	As a result of this	3 vegetation has also been changing. e.g. In Canada, the agricultural cropline has shifted 50 to 100 miles northward.
—	has also been affected	4 The distribution of wildlife e.g. many European animals moving northwards into Scandinavia.
the melting of glaciers	(largely) due to	5 The sea has been rising at a rapidly increasing rate, e.g. in the last 18 years it has risen by about 6 inches.

2 A variety of answers are possible. The most likely ones are listed below.
  (1) caused/resulted in/led to (2) because/as/since (3) because of/as a result of/due to/on account of/ owing to/through (4) consequently,/ Therefore,/ As a result,/Because of this,/etc. (5) caused/ resulted in/led to (6) cause of/reason for

Unit 10   Key

Notes on the Exercises

The different columns in the Scale of Qualification in the Structure and Vocabulary Aid need to be looked at and carefully compared. It would be useful to look again at the Structure and Vocabulary Aid to Unit 8 (Qualification of Comparison).

Stage 2

Reference is made to predictive statements or predictions. Such generalised comments are based upon past experience and information. You can see, therefore, that there may be a close link between the past and the future (this will be important for verb tenses).

Answers to the Exercises

Stage 1

2

Quantity	Frequency	Probability
all minority majority a little most a number	usually seldom generally	likelihood undoubtedly likely will not definitely

Stage 2

1   Some flexibility is possible with the answers but there should be a range of quantity qualifications used, e.g. *most, the majority of, many, (a) few*.

2   A range of probability qualifications will need to be used, e.g. *probable, likely, possible, unlikely*. Each one may be further qualified if necessary by adding *very* in front of it.

3   Some variation is possible with the quantity qualifications but the answers should be similar to these:

> *A minority of* students were *rarely* able to obtain their coursebooks from libraries.
> *The majority of . . . sometimes . . .*
> *A number of . . . often . . .*
> *A few . . . always . . .*

Stage 3

1   The following words should be underlined. They are given here in the order in which they appear in the text.

> may; possible; can be; may; may be; often; suggests; quite; may; can be; perhaps; may; tend to; may; often; most frequently; seem; can be; not . . . necessarily; possible; suggest; It appears; can . . . be; do not seem

Unit 11   Key

Notes on the Exercises

This unit is useful for practising different expressions associated with visual information, viz. histogram, chart, graph, table.

Stage 1

The plural of *axis* is *axes*. It is wrong to write *from the chart 1*. It should be either: *from chart 1* or *from the chart*.

The organisation of information is important. Normally there is a progression from big to small (or vice versa) or a big/small contrast.

Sequencing markers or connectives may be used, i.e. *first, next, then, followed by, finally*.

In Chart 1 the approximate percentages are:

	%			1997 millions
	1800	1900	1997	
Asia	65	57	60	3,539
Africa	11	8	13	758
Europe	21	25	12	729
Latin America and Caribbean	2	4	8	492
North America	0.7	5	5	302
Oceania	0.2	0.4	0.5	29
1997 world population: 5,849 million				

(*Source: Social Trends: 28*, 1998. Office for National Statistics, London: Stationery Office.)

Stage 2

1 In Graph 1 the actual figures are:

Year	Total in thousands
1811	13,368
1821	15,472
1831	17,835
1841	20,183
1851	22,259
1861	24,525
1871	27,431
1881	31,015
1891	34,264
1901	38,237
1911	42,082
1921	44,027
1931	46,038
1951	50,225
1961	52,709
1971	55,515
1981	55,848
1991	56,467

(*Source*: *Whitaker's Almanack*, 1996. J. Whitaker & Sons, London.)

Useful introductory phrases are:

During the period 1811 to 1991 . . .
From 1811 to 1991 . . .
Since 1811 . . .
For 180 years, from 1811 to 1991, . . .

2 For predictions the verbs will be in the future tense or/and will involve a qualification of probability.

It is perhaps necessary to comment that we assume that the trend shown in the graph will continue in a similar way. The basis of any calculations used in predicting a trend should be indicated in the answer.

Stage 3
Different visual information is provided in order to give further practice. Only the most significant/ interesting items should be commented on.
For an additional exercise in trends, the Stage 1 chart of the distribution of the world's population could be described, showing the trends of the continents over the period of nearly 200 years.

Answers to the Exercises

Stage 1

1 Suggested answer:
As can be seen from the chart, Europe had the second-largest population in 1900. In fact, Europe accounted for 25% of the world's population in that year, in second place behind Asia's 57%. It had a considerably larger population than Africa, in third place with only 8%.

Stage 2

1 Suggested answer:
As can be seen from the graph, during the period 1811 to 1991 there was a steady increase in the population growth in the UK. At the beginning of the period the population was 13.3 million and by the end it had grown to 56.4 million. The fastest growth was from 1811 to 1911; thereafter, the growth was more gradual.

Unit 13   Key

Notes on the Exercises
The exercises in this unit can be used for revising some of the language functions practised in earlier units, e.g. definitions (what is infant mortality?), exemplification, comparison and contrast.

Stage 2
It may be of interest to see how the writer concluded the passage 'Advantages and Disadvantages of the Lecturing Method' in Unit 12 Stage 1. The survey was concluded thus:

An aspect of lecturing rarely, if ever, mentioned by its critics is its efficiency. With the aid of microphones and closed circuit television it is possible to reach large audiences within one building; and, as we know from national television, lectures of great interest, employing expensive visual aids and a high standard of preparation, can be made available to millions. Moreover, videotapes may enable other audiences to see and discuss the same programmes subsequently at times convenient in their own courses. Had there been little else to say in their favour, these advantages of economy and availability would certainly ensure their continuation, but even without the aid of television, lecturing is still an economical method.

(Notice the use of inversion at the beginning of the final sentence – *Had there been . . .* This is used to give greater emphasis to the advantages.)

Stage 3

The concept of a correlation can be utilised here. A correlation is a shared relationship or causal connection between items, e.g. *There is a high correlation between unemployment and crime.*

The cause of the accidents is not given in Table 3.

Answers to the Exercises

Stage 1

1 The introductory paragraph is poor because it does not say which country is being discussed or what the essay will contain or the order in which it will be discussed. It plunges straight into emotional and exaggerated statements about different forms of pollution. This must create an unfavourable impression on the reader and will probably prejudice him/her against the rest of the essay.

2 The language is more controlled and not as emotive and exaggerated as in **1**. In the final two sentences it indicates what will be covered in the essay and it refers to the conclusion.

4 Both paragraphs are possible introductions. Personal preference will play some part in the choice.
   a The first paragraph is very short and, perhaps, does not tell us much. It is not good style to put *of course* in the first sentence.
   b The second paragraph will be considered by some to be the best as it sets out precisely, and in sequence, what the essay will include

and uses linking words: *starting with . . . then . . . after this . . . finally . . .*

Stage 2

Notes for possible conclusions (to be written as a paragraph):
a In favour of exams:
   1 Often not the only way of assessing a student; often used in conjunction with other methods.
   2 Not a perfect system, but the best available.
b Against exams:
   1 There must be a more effective way of assessing ability.
   2 A profitable business for examining bodies!
Some of the main points that you agree with can be included in the paragraph as a lead-in to your own views.

Stage 3

1 Some possible comments that can be made in your conclusion are as follows:
   Generally, it can be concluded that there is a high correlation between infant mortality rate and life expectancy. In general, countries that have a high infant mortality rate have a lower life expectancy.
   Almost without exception, women have a higher life expectancy than men. Overall, both men and women live longer in 1990–1995 than they did in 1950–1955. There are some regional variations in both infant mortality rates and life expectancy.

Unit 14 Key

Notes on the Exercises

Useful information about academic vocabulary, in the form of university word lists, is contained in: *Teaching and Learning Vocabulary* by I.S.P. Nation, 1990 (Newbury House/Harper-Collins, New York)

Answers to the Exercises

Stage 1

2 aF bI cI dF eF fF gI hI iF jI
3 Suggested answers:
   1 It was said that it was unsatisfactory.
   2 It seemed that the lecture was very difficult to understand.
   3 They need to discover how to conduct a survey of elderly people's opinions of young children.

4 The results appeared to be better than expected.
5 It was reported that the answer was not known by any of the students.
6 It was said that one man was very unhappy at being alone.

4 1 A survey has shown that many lecturers seem to use the terms 'seminars' and 'tutorials' frequently interchangeably.
   2 There is an assumption that the rate of inflation may not increase next year.
   3 It is said that reading is most effective when it has a particular purpose.
   4 Perhaps the answer to problems is to be found in asking the right questions.
   5 Many countries appear to disagree on the interpretation of democracy.

Stage 2

1   a6   b3   c5   d2   e8   f7   g1   h4

3   a   A dictionary definition. This is from the *Longman Dictionary of Contemporary English*.

   b   An explanation by an economist. Spoken formally in a lecture or written (in a text book).

   c   A proverb – about the effects of poverty.

   d   A specialist economics dictionary definition. (From the *Penguin Dictionary of Economics* by Graham Bannock, R.E. Baxter and Evan Davis. Penguin Books, London. Fifth Edition, 1992.)

   e   A spoken explanation by an educated adult.

   f   Informally spoken, or a letter written to a friend (or relative). It uses euphemisms (*badly off/hard up*).

   g   From literature. From the Preface to the play *Major Barbara* (1907) by G.B. Shaw (1856–1950).

   h   From a history text. From *The Common People: 1746–1946* by G.D.H. Cole and Raymond Postgate. Methuen, London. Second edition, 1956)

Stage 3

Suggested answer:

Some research suggests (James, 1988) that learners of English appear to find that writing is the most difficult skill for them to master. There are three main types of error that learners frequently might make.

The most serious type of error may lead to a misunderstanding or a total breakdown in communication. There are many causes of this: one of the biggest is the use of translation from the mother tongue. By translating word for word, the student may employ the wrong sentence patterns and the wrong vocabulary. Another cause is choosing to write long and complex sentences with an excessive number of subordinate clauses. The longer the sentence, the greater is the likelihood of making mistakes and failing to communicate the meaning. Consequently, in the early stages of their writing, the advice to students is that they should not write sentences which are longer than three lines.

Some comments about types of error:

–   a year is needed for the reference
–   *thing* and *do* are too vague
–   contractions (*they've*) are inappropriate
–   avoid *you* – keep it impersonal
–   small numbers should be put into words
–   a number of the words are inappropriate: more formal language is needed
–   a number of statements need to be qualified

Unit 15   Key

Answers to the Exercises

Stage 1

Suggested answers:

1   Smith and Jones (1991) discovered that the situation had . . .

2   The problems caused by seminars were observed by Brown and White (1994) . . .

3   The conclusion of James and Harris (1984), that there was a need for note-taking practice, led to the development of appropriate exercises.

4   Dunkel (1988) has pointed out that there is a close link between taking very brief notes and the usefulness of notes. This observation was supported by the report of research findings by Chaudron, Loschky and Cook (1994).

Stage 2

1   The first sentence.

2   Some possible comments are as follows:

–   it contains instances of paraphrase/changing some of the vocabulary
–   it focuses on the main points
–   it omits examples and expansion

4   Suggested summary (others are possible):
The most favoured pastimes in Britain are home-based, with television being the most popular, including video, followed by listening to the radio.

Stage 3

1   Suggested answer:
There are two main advantages of tourism (Johnson, 1971), one of which is economic, i.e. local employment, and the other is the support it provides for local services. However, there are also three major disadvantages (Walker, 1982): firstly, erosion, then traffic congestion and, thirdly, pollution from traffic and people.

Unit 16 Key

Answers to the Exercises

Stage 1

1 LIST A
   1 Davey, A.C.
   2 Davey, A.M.
   3 Davidson, D.
   4 Davidson, G.D.
   5 Davies, C.T.
   6 Davies, C.W.
   7 Davis, A.
   8 Davy, A.
   9 Dawes, C.G.
   10 Dawkins, R.
   11 Dawson, E.
   12 Day, D.A.

   LIST B
   1 Jackson, J.
   2 James, C.V.
   3 James, D.V.
   4 James, K.
   5 Johns, A.M.
   6 Johns, C.
   7 Johns, T.F.
   8 Johnson, K.
   9 Johnson, R.
   10 Johnston, S.A.
   11 Jones, C.
   12 Jones, J.F.

2 The bibliography below has been corrected with
   some comments about the errors.

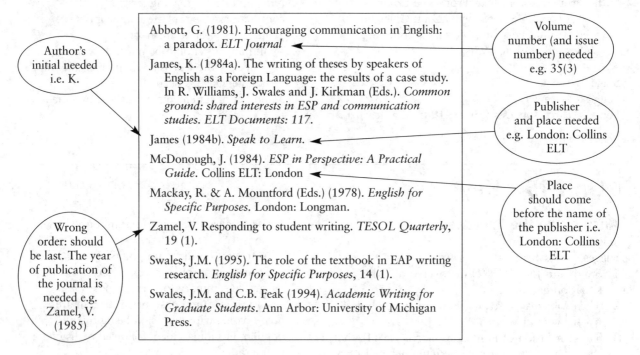

Comments:
McDonough comes before Mackay (McD = MacD).
Swales, J.M. (1995) comes before Swales and Feak
(1994) even though it is a year later – because the
names of authors alone come before two or three
names together.

Stage 2

1 There are two sources for quotations:
   – Beard and Hartley, 1984
   – Hartley and Knapper, 1984
   There are four sources for paraphrases:
   – Smith, 1982
   – Jordan, 1993
   – Hartley and Knapper, 1984
   – Northedge, 1990

2 Suggested answer:

Plagiarism and its History

To plagiarize may be defined as *to take words, ideas, etc. from someone else's work and use them in your work, as if they were your own ideas* (Longman Dictionary, 1995). The origin of plagiarism is noted in McArthur (1992) as coming from the obsolete noun *plagiary* meaning a kidnapper or a kidnapping, theft or a thief of ideas. This, in turn, came from the Latin word *plagiarius* meaning a kidnapper or a literary thief.

The first recorded use of *plagiary* was in the late 16th century. Both *plagiary* and *plagiarism* are included in the 18th century dictionaries of Nathaniel Bailey and Samuel Johnson.

For some students, plagiarism may be unintentional, caused by their lack of awareness of the academic convention in English of acknowledging all sources in their writing. For this reason, many study guides and other books for students give advice, examples and ways in which sources should be cited (e.g. Hamp-Lyons and Courter, 1984; Leki, 1989; Waters and Waters, 1995). One article in particular clearly sets out the format for a bibliography, showing the different layout necessary for books, journals and other papers (Lynch and McGrath, 1993).

References:

Hamp-Lyons, L. and K.B. Courter (1984). *Research Matters*. Cambridge, Mass.: Newbury House.

Leki, I. (1989). *Academic Writing*. New York: St. Martin's Press.

Longman Dictionary of Contemporary English (1995: 3rd edition). Harlow, Essex: Longman Group Ltd.

Lynch, T. and I. McGrath (1993). Teaching bibliographic documentation skills. *English for Specific Purposes*, 12 (3).

McArthur, T.(Ed.) (1992). *The Oxford Companion to the English Language*. Oxford: Oxford University Press.

Waters, M. and A. Waters (1995). *Study Tasks in English*. Cambridge: Cambridge University Press.

Unit 17   Key

Notes on the Exercises

Stage 1

Additional topics, suitable for constructing questionnaires to obtain personal views, are as follows:

- Participation in sports and games (outdoor and indoor)
- Social activities and hobbies
- Students' backgrounds and future plans for studies and work

Unit 18   Key

Answers to the Exercises

Stage 1

1 a Table 4 *shows* that most of *these* accidents *occur* to young *children*.

b Each worker *pays* a small *sum/amount* of money which is deducted *from his/her* salary (or: *their salaries*).

c Specialist doctors in hospitals *can be divided into* surgeons *who* operate *on* the body and *other* specialists *who* act as *consultants*.

d The *number of schools* grew gradually *until* (cf. till) 1965 and then *the* number *rose* suddenly.

e When a country *applies* for *foreign aid, it is* because it has *not* enough resources of *its* own.

f *It* is bigger and (*much*) better in country A *than* in country B.

g *On* the other hand, *if* we *look at* the table of *information*, we will see *these* facts.

h The problem *was solved* (or: the *problems* were *solved*) by *the* introduction of *machinery* (or: *machines*).

2 a made (had made)   d raised (had raised)

b done   e rose

c told (had told)

3 a borrow
  b advice . . . choose
  c their . . . affected . . . weather
  d principal . . . imminent . . . two
  e mathematics . . . politics . . . logical . . . latter

Stage 2

1 1C 2B 3C 4D 5A 6C 7B 8A 9D 10A
   11C 12B

2 a absence   k medicine
   b accommodation   l millennium
   c argument   m misspelled (misspelt)
   d achieve   n occurred
   e criticism   o pronunciation
   f disappeared   p research
   g embarrassed   q referred (or: refereed)
   h exaggerated   r successful
   i grammar   s transferred
   j gratefully   t withhold

3 a acquired   h professional
   b beginning   i received
   d conscience   l weather or whether
   f innovation

4 Some variations to the following may be possible. Check with your teacher.
   When a student goes to study in another country (,) some initial problems may be caused by differences in academic conventions or customs. Even the academic staff's titles can be confusing: for example, the title (') professor (') does not have exactly the same status everywhere. Differences can occur in English-speaking countries (,) e.g. U(.)K(.), U(.)S(.)A(.), Canada, Australia, New Zealand, etc. In some it may mean the most senior of academics, in others simply a university teacher.
   Some students may be uncertain how to use titles. They may ask themselves the question: 'How do I address a professor when I meet one? Do I say, for example, "Good morning, Professor Smith . . ."?'

Unit 19   Key

Notes on the Exercises

In some of the external/public exams, as well as in college/university internal exams, a fairly common type of question involves the problem-solution pattern. In other words, a problem is posed in the question. Your answer needs to comment on the problem or difficulty and to try to suggest possible answers to it, if appropriate referring to evidence from other writing or research. Some kind of discussion of the possible answers is usually needed. Practice is given in this in Stage 2.

Answers to the Exercises

Stage 1

1 You should have read everything before writing anything. Consequently, you should only write the answers to numbers 1, 2 and 3 (as stated in number 11), i.e. your name and date of birth.

2 a Three hours
   b Three
   c Yes – 1a or 1b
   d Twelve (including the choices of a or b)
   e At least one i.e. 1a or 1b
   f No
   g No. a or b
   h One hour

Stage 2

Various answers to the writing tasks are possible and need to be checked with your teacher. Some of the writing tasks and Structure and Vocabulary Aids from previous units (especially Units 12 and 13) will be useful in these kinds of questions which usually involve description, discussion, analysis and evaluation, together with your own views.

Notes

Notes

Notes

Acknowledgements

Grateful acknowledgements are made to the following for ideas:

'What Are Science Students Expected To Write?' – J. Friedrichs & H. D. Pierson – in *ELT Journal*, Vol. XXXV No. 4, July 1981. 'Essay Examination Prompts and the Teaching of Academic Writing' – D. Horowitz – in *English for Specific Purposes*, Vol. 5 No. 2, 1986. *Answering Examination Questions* – P. M. Howe – Collins ELT 1983. *Writing Theses and Dissertations* – J. P. Ryan – University of Manchester 1982. 'The care and maintenance of hedges' – J. Skelton – in *ELT Journal*, Vol. 42 No. 1, January 1988. 'Examining Examination Papers' – J. Swales – in *English Language Research Journal*, No. 3, 1982. 'Hedging in Academic Writing and EAP Textbooks' – Ken Hyland – in *English for Specific Purposes*, Vol. 13 No. 3, 1994.

We are indebted to the following for permission to reproduce copyright material:
BBC Books for an adapted extract based on 'Adjusting to Higher Education' in *Illustrated Economics* by Peter Donaldson; Harper & Row Ltd for adapted extracts from *Teaching and Learning in Higher Education* by R. Beard & J. Hartley, 4th edition, 1984; Pan Books for an adapted extract from *The Story of Language* by C.L. Barber, 1964; Penguin Books Ltd for adapted extracts from *Teaching and Learning in Higher Education* by Ruth Beard, 2nd edition, 1972 and for an adapted extract from *Ornithology – An Introduction* by Austin L. Rand, 1974; Thames & Hudson Ltd for an extract from *The Doomsday Book* by G. Rattray Taylor, 1970.

We have been unable to trace the copyright holder of *The Book of British Birds* published by Drive Publications, 1969, and would appreciate any information which would enable us to do so.

The tables and diagrams in Units 3, 8, 11 and 13 are based upon data from the following publications which are gratefully acknowledged: *Annual Abstract of Statistics*, 1998, Stationery Office, London; *Chambers World Gazetteer*, 1988; *Philip's Geographical Digest*, 1996; *Social Trends*, 1998, Stationery Office, London; *Whitaker's Almanack*, 1998.

Photographs

We are grateful to the following for permission to reproduce copyright photographs:
Addison Wesley Longman page 53 (Trevor Clifford); BBC Natural History Unit pages 45 (Mike Wilkes/sparrow), 59 (Chris O'Reilly/silver birch), 82 (Charlie Hamilton James/bird); Bruce Coleman Ltd pages 39 (Dennis Green/bird), 45 (Werner Layer/crow, George McCarthy/skull, Hans Reinhard/eagle), 59 (Johnny Johnson/glacier); Collections pages 16 (Paul Bryans), 66 (Nigel French); Greg Evans International page 78; Mary Evans Picture Library page 27; Format page 107 (Jacky Chapman); Robert Harding Picture Library page 95 (Martyn F. Chillmaid); Hulton Getty page 29 (Vienna University, Bologna University); The Image Bank page 120 (Terry Williams); Network Photographers page 71 (Gideon Mendel); Panos Pictures page 61 (Ron Gilling/famine); Pictor International pages 29 (Christ Church), 52, 76, 85, 105; Rex Features Ltd pages 28, 39 (Simon Walker/Times/Sergeant), 43 (Alexandra Caminada/primary class), 60 (Stuart Clarke/traffic), 61 (flood), 64 (Dave Hogan), 82 (traffic), 107 (Jaime Abecasis); Science Photolibrary page 51 (Earth Satellite Corporation/satellite picture); Tony Stone Images pages 59 (Robert Stahl/spruce trees), 89 (David Young Wolff), 90 (Simon Norfolk); Telegraph Colour Library page 100 (Daniel Allan); John Walmsley pages 43 (comprehensive school, grammar school), 66.
Picture research by Diane Jones.